What readers say about '52 Ways to Grow Your Business'

"Brilliant!"

"A great little book to keep your business and ambitions on track in tough times. I often start to read in-depth marketing books and read them far too fast. In a hurry to get through the long-winded theory, I end up skipping over details and loose the point. With this book there is no way of that happening. An excellent balance of examples, practical ideas and plain old common sense, written in straightforward, concise language that I found easy to relate to."

"Highly recommended."

"This book will be a great tool to keep me focused as my own business develops and stay true to what I was aiming for when I started out."

"The thing I really like about *52 Ways to Grow your Business* is its simple no-nonsense style. Alastair Campbell is clearly speaking from experience; the ideas are very practical. We are immediately looking at several of them for our business. As well as marketing ideas, there are tips around mindset which I really like too. Not to be missed."

"A brilliant reminder of things we should be doing that we've either forgotten or didn't know about in the first place."

"This book provides a valuable set of tools that will bring real benefits to your business – big or small. I particularly liked the chapters on Time Wasting Habits (how true) and What Your Company Stands For – excellent."

"I read this book in one sitting and have gained several ideas for my own business. A great 'business bible' to revisit time and time again when you need ideas and inspiration."

"This book will help your business to perform in a way that delivers results. It's an easy read with practical ideas and suggestions for every business and sector and has left me with several marketing ideas to implement. I would recommend the book to anyone who owns a business."

"A very readable and relevant book with loads of really practical ideas for anyone who runs a business to use or adapt in order to improve how they approach existing and future customers."

"I have been running my business for 12 years now and I found myself saying 'I like that idea – I will try it out!'"

What readers say about 'The Marketing Launchpad'

"This short, punchy little book is easy to read and urges the reader to turn the page. Many such publications can contain boring or irrelevant sections but this little gem was ALL relevant for me and I would recommend the book to anyone struggling to gain some focus in their marketing strategy. Marketing isn't rocket science but can sometimes appear so. This book takes away the hard edges from the problem and provides easy-to-digest solutions."

"I'm in the process of moving my business to larger premises and wanted some marketing guidance to help maximise the potential for growth. I was recommended [The Marketing Launchpad] by a friend and was delighted to read it. It really inspired and motivated me with its many practical and straightforward ideas and tips."

"I take [The Marketing Launchpad] with me wherever I go – it's my little marketing guidebook for every occasion."

"I've recently read *The Marketing Launchpad*, and I think it's great. I like the fact that it's based around six key principles, and I was able to read them in about half an hour each. It is well set out and focuses on the key aspects of marketing for small business. It is very well targeted – so is probably not ideal for marketing people in big companies. But for people running SMEs, it is invaluable and a real easy read."

"*The Marketing Launchpad* is an easy read and has left me with several marketing ideas to follow up on and implement. Some of these I'd been thinking about doing but not sure how, and this book has given me some direction. Others – especially niche marketing – I'd not thought about before."

"With only being a small business, it is hard to know where to start with regards to marketing. Reading *The Market Launchpad* has given me food for through and will help me moving forward and help my business grow."

"*The Marketing Launchpad* is an easy, dynamic read which gives an invaluable insight in to how to get the best results from your marketing. Having read the book, I am looking at all our past marketing in a new light, which is not very flattering, to be honest, as I think that like many businesses our marketing wasn't really something we gave much time to. Will all the ideas in the book work in our business? I don't know for sure, but I'm sure that if I employ the ideas laid out and give some proper thought to our marketing, I'll be able to develop a more successful marketing strategy overall and this time I'll be able to monitor it. A great marketing starting point. I can't imagine that there isn't something in this book to help everybody."

❖ *The Marketing Launchpad* is available to order via Amazon and other online retailers, or direct from the publisher.

52 WAYS TO GROW YOUR BUSINESS

An 'idea a week' to generate enquiries, improve conversion rates and retain your existing clients

ALASTAIR CAMPBELL

MOSAÏQUEPRESS

Published by
MOSAÏQUE PRESS
70 Priory Road
Kenilworth, Warwickshire CV8 1LQ
www.mosaïquepress.co.uk

Copyright © 2012 Alastair Campbell

The right of Alastair Campbell to be identified as the author of this work has been asserted in accordance with the Copyright, Designs and Patents Act 1998.

All rights reserved. No part of this publication may be reproduced or utilised in any form or by any means, electronic or mechanical, including photocopying, recording or by any information storage and retrieval system without the permission in writing from Mosaïque Press.

Cover design by Oliver Betts from Beta Graphic

Printed in the UK

ISBN 978-1-906852-15-3

*Dedicated to my wonderful wife, Helen,
and my two wonderful boys, Robbie and Ben.
Thanks for being so patient with me.*

ALASTAIR CAMPBELL

CONTENTS

Foreword by Karen Harewood	13
Introduction	15
1. Begin with the end in mind	21
2. Focus on what your customers want, not what you want to sell	24
3. Develop repeat business	26
4 Create niche products for niche areas	29
5. Don't aim to be the cheapest, aim to be the best	31
6. Watch your language: use the 'you' word, not the 'we' word	33
7. Write to people or companies you would like to work with	36
8. Build up a database of the big fish that you would like to work with	38
9. Attend regular networking events	40
10. Go to where your customers go	45

11. Develop the philosophy of 'next'	47
12. Everybody connected with your business is involved in marketing it	49
13. Salesmanship is the transfer of enthusiasm to another person	51
14. Find the gaps	53
15. Take time to explain to your team what you want from them and where you are going	56
16. Can a successful product be transferred into a parallel market?	60
17. Send out press releases regularly	62
18. Send out article pitches regularly	67
19. What does your company stand for?	70
20. Improve your customers' perception of you via sponsorship of the right event	72
21. Always ask where people heard about your company when they first enquire	74
22. Create a newsletter for customers and prospects	77
23. Think 'how can I help' rather than 'how can I sell'	79
24. Learn from your competitors	81
25. Keep in regular contact with your existing customers	83
26. Create a 'sticky' message to make it easier for your customers to tell people about you	85

27. Spend money on things that matter — 88
28. Keep studying your area of expertise and other areas of business that will help you to grow — 90
29. Create a system for gathering testimonials from satisfied customers — 92
30. Your company should be improving every month — 95
31. Think back to what has already worked for you in the past — 97
32. Don't rely on words alone — 99
33. Ask your customers what they like and don't like about your company — 101
34. Ask your ex-customers why they left — 103
35. Discover your dangerous time-wasting habits — 105
36. Produce good quality but don't obsess over making everything 'perfect' — 107
37. Test everything you do to see what works about it and what doesn't — 109
38. Only sell products or services that you believe in — 111
39. Do more of what you are passionate about and delegate what you can't do or hate doing — 113
40. Find ways to keep inspired — 115
41. Watch your energy levels and overall health — 117

42. Enter awards and display your trophies where people will see them — 119
43. Find people you trust to give you ideas and advice — 122
44. Use people in your marketing material (nobody wants to eat in an empty restaurant) — 125
45. Put action into your exhibitions — 127
46. Watch out for poor language within your organisation — 130
47. Metaphors are a great way to explain difficult or complex ideas — 132
48. Making any decision is usually better than making no decision — 134
49. Enter into joint ventures with related but non-competing businesses — 138
50. Write a booklet of tips — 141
51. Revisit your past customers: they are a potential goldmine — 145
52. Always give more than you promised and look for ways of delivering added value — 147

A parting gift to you — 151
About the author — 153

FOREWORD by Karen Harewood

English 800m Champion 2011
www.yourliferules.co.uk

ALASTAIR CAMPBELL has made it his business since 2003 to help his clients to grow and reach their potential by becoming more effective with their marketing.

As a business-owning athlete, I have always been fascinated by the parallels between growing a successful business and creating success in sport. Both require a mindset that incorporates a desire to achieve and a willingness to commit to a course of action that will bridge the gap from where we are to where we want to be.

When I made the decision to become an athlete at the relatively mature age of 27, I had to find a coach who knew more about what it took to become an athlete than I did. What Charlie McConnell taught me over the following two years transformed me from a fun runner into an international 800m athlete representing Great Britain at World and European Championships. He showed me how to bridge the gap from average to elite.

The information in this book offers you the same opportunity for your business. The selection of activities and tasks which Alastair Campbell presents in these pages are ones he has found to be effective in delivering growth to businesses across many sectors — from start-up firms to long-established firms.

Bridging the gap from mediocre to great, or from great to exceptional doesn't have to be as hard as you might think. It is simply a matter of knowing the right things to do, and then doing them with consistency.

What *52 Ways to Grow Your Business* offers is a set of tools you can use to build your own bridge. These are the 'right things' to be doing and if you do them with some consistency, it is inevitable that you will 'bridge that gap'.

I was fortunate to have found Charlie and you are just as fortunate to have found Alastair. I wish you every success as he coaches you to greater business growth.

Karen Harewood

INTRODUCTION

If one great idea can transform your business, imagine what 52 ideas can do.

THIS book is written for business owners who don't want to read a lot of marketing theory. It's for people who would rather pick up some quick ideas that they can introduce today than spend four months learning about how they can alter their business tomorrow.

People like you.

Perhaps like you don't usually have time to read business or marketing books. But I'm sure you do have time to read just a few hundred words each week that will give you a powerful idea, each one of which is capable of making a profound difference to the profitability of your business.

In these pages you will read about profitable ideas on marketing, PR and motivational strategies – ideas that are designed to give you plenty of suggestions on growing your business quickly and inexpensively.

Sometimes it's useful to take inspiration from ideas that have worked for other people before you. That's where this book comes in. It contains 52 ideas that people have used to grow their businesses. Most of them are linked in some way to the book's three main topics: marketing, PR and advertising. Some of them are more about the mindset that you need to adopt as a business owner. But all of them could work for you if you adopt them and you are serious about business growth.

In my view, growing a business takes place in one of four ways:

1. **Attraction** – attracting new customers
2. **Conversion** – converting those interested prospects
3. **Retention** – retaining your customers for longer
4. **Extension** – extending the relationship with your customers so that some of them will become ambassadors for your company.

If you are able to achieve all four in your business, it could take off rapidly and grow at a rate that you dictate yourself.

But most people don't do this. Perhaps they focus all their business activity only on acquiring new customers. If so, they are likely to be disappointed. The customers may cross the road and walk into your shop, or visit your website, or come into your restaurant. However, once there, they may not buy and if they do, there's no guarantee they'll return.

Providing an excellent service, good value and looking for

ways to always improve the service you offer is essential if you're serious about business growth.

This book contains a number of stories, facts, anecdotes and ideas that I have picked up in the course of speaking to business owners over 20 years. When I first entered the advertising world in the late 1980s, marketing was a very different place to what it is now. Not only did e-mail and websites not exist, I can remember the creative department at the agency where I worked fighting with a client because they didn't want to include a telephone number.

These days, thankfully, the emphasis is far more on specific immediate measurable results that can be achieved from an advertising campaign than it was back then. Many things have changed over the last two decades; however, fundamental principles of marketing have remained unchanged for more than a century. Offer excellent value, think about the benefits that your product or service offers, and place your customer first are universal truths that are unlikely to go out of fashion, ever.

I'm sure that some of the 52 ideas you read over the coming pages will be useful to you straight away in your business. Others you may wish to think about for a while and perhaps adapt to your own needs and purposes. Some you may disagree with. However, if you do disagree with an idea contained in these pages, think about what your objection is. Do you dislike it because it goes against conventional wisdom? If so, I would urge you to consider it carefully before discarding it.

You may be the sort of person who, to get the most out of a book like this, should read it all through, making notes in the margin for the ideas that you could see working in your business.

Each time you read one of these ideas, ask yourself: "Could I introduce and take action on this idea today?" If the answer is yes, don't waste any time. Either delegate the idea or take action yourself. Don't wait until you've read the whole book: as the idea seizes you, take action immediately.

Alternatively, if you don't have much time, simply ready one new idea each week and then take action on that idea over the next seven days. Can you imagine what will happen to your business if you introduce just one idea a week? Could you double its size over the next year? I see no reason why not.

One of the things that never ceases to surprise me is how many great ideas people have, and how few of them they actually use. Better to be somebody who has only had a few good ideas in their life and has done something with them, than be the person who has hundreds of ideas but never takes action. Remember, ideas for growing your business will only make you money if you introduce them and do something with them. An idea that is unused is as useless as no idea at all.

However, I am sure that if you are the sort of person who has decided to buy this book, you are the sort of person who is more likely to take action than the average business owner.

I have designed this book so that each section can be read quickly, the information absorbed and the appropriate action taken. Rather than write a book with 15 or 20 chapters, I thought I would write a book where each idea is only a page or so long. That means you can read an idea while you're waiting for a meeting in little more than the time it would take to read a short newspaper article. Or, if you're a bedtime reader, even if you're very tired, you can still read one of these ideas before turning off the light. Any time during your busy day when you can find a few minutes, you can read an idea.

Who knows, some of these ideas might be worth hundreds of thousands of pounds to you over the coming decades if you introduce them. Perhaps that alone will encourage you to carry on reading and, more importantly, to continue introducing these ideas within your business.

I hope you enjoy the book; I hope it will introduce you to some profitable new ideas. I'd love to know how you get on introducing them. Let me know how you do. And if you have any of your own ideas that you think are worth sharing, do drop me an e-mail at alastair@idealmarketingcompany.com.

One final thing. Apart from the first idea, and the very last idea, there is no particular order to the material contained within these pages. I have deliberately decided not to have a section on PR, a section on direct mail etc. Instead I have mixed them all up so you will never know what to expect next. That way, I hope you will be surprised by some of the ideas that otherwise you might have skipped over because you felt you were already very familiar with a particular subject.

Thank you again for buying this book. I hope it repays your investment hundreds of times over.

1
BEGIN WITH THE END IN MIND

THINK ABOUT how you want your company to develop and plan accordingly.

When you look at the most successful companies, it is clear that they have not just happened. They have been planned in the same way that an architect will plan a skyscraper or a cathedral. While it is rare for managing directors to know exactly where they want their business to end up, they usually have a clear idea about areas where it will work, the type of customer service they wish to offer, how the structure of the business will be built and a number of other key points.

Imagine a scenario where you decide you would like to build your own house. You wouldn't just ask the builder to deposit several tons of bricks, wood and concrete in some spare land and start putting the house together. First of all, you would decide where the house was going to be. Then you would decide what the house might look like, how many rooms it will have, different aspects around price and specification etc.

Building a business should happen in exactly the same way. First of all, you plan the aspects of the business on paper; then you work out how you can make those ideas and dreams into your reality.

Some businesses are built around a single powerful idea such as 'a car on every driveway in America', which is how Henry Ford saw the Ford Motor Company when cars were very much the preserve of the super-wealthy. He used this simple and singular vision in the early days of the company to drive everything that he created. For Ford, it was about improving production techniques and making cars cheaply enough so that they could be enjoyed by the majority of the population. At that time, he could have had no idea that cars would become quite so popular worldwide or indeed of the many advances that would happen to the various technologies that go into cars. This strong vision was enough to drive his business and the entire car manufacturing industry forward.

If we do not know where we are going when we set up a business, then how can we expect our staff to follow our idea? How can we expect to communicate with passion and enthusiasm to our customers?

Every great business usually starts with a simple idea and a strong vision to drive it forward. So decide now where you would like your company to go. Are you looking to sell your business in 10 years time? Are you looking for it to provide comfortable regular income with minimal fuss? Are you looking to pass it on to your family one day? What type of profit are you looking to take out the business? What sort of turnover are you looking for? Which markets do you want to operate in? Which parts of the country do you want your offices to open in? These are all important questions to consider even in the very early stages of running a business. They will help you overcome difficult decisions and make you focus on what the business really should be about – for you.

Without absolute clarity for what you want your business to be, it becomes all too easy to do what other people suggest and end up forming a company which grows in a direction that you don't want it to grow. Be clear from the beginning - but of course be flexible when opportunities arise. Trees grow in one direction, but they are flexible enough to bend with the wind. Stay flexible so you are able to make the most of relevant opportunities - and turn down those which are ultimately going to take you further away from your final destination.

> Your mind, while blessed with permanent memory, is cursed with lousy recall. Written goals provide clarity. By documenting your dreams, you must think about the process of achieving them."
>
> —Gary Ryan Blair

ALASTAIR CAMPBELL

2
FOCUS ON WHAT YOUR CUSTOMERS WANT, NOT WHAT YOU WANT TO SELL

THE ECONOMIES of the world are littered with the skeletons of industries which decided to sell to customers what they produced, rather than what the customer wanted.

I recently heard a BBC Radio 4 documentary on the British potteries industry. For a long time, British pottery was known throughout the world for its high quality and indeed highly efficient production techniques. The documentary was focusing on one particular factory which had undergone something of a resurgence after being bought and brought back from the brink of bankruptcy – for the sixth time.

The production manager was explaining the different types of plates and cups that they sold. He explained the process that the company underwent to decide what new items were going to be sold. It had nothing to do with what the customers wanted, or indeed what had sold well the previous year. Instead the designers and owners of the factory decided what would go on sale that year and the sales force would then be told to sell to them as best they could. Sadly for this factory and many others, this course of action led to financial disaster. It meant items were being sold not on popularity but on a whim and a guess. It brought a once-great industry to its knees.

In the meantime, markets in other parts of the world were copying the production techniques pioneered by the British and were conducting extensive market research into what customers wanted. The result was faster delivery times and cheaper dishes which suited the customers' diverse requirements. Meanwhile the British industry, by refusing to listen to what the customer wanted, was doomed to failure.

Many companies will develop products which they think are interesting without ever asking for customer feedback. Names and products aren't tested before the product is launched into the market. While it isn't always possible to gauge public reaction accurately, it is always a good idea to respond to public wishes. Trends can be set for people to follow, but it is usually a good idea to measure the mood of the public and ask direct questions to see what people are likely to demand in the future.

One of the easiest ways to do that is to monitor what is currently selling well and what is selling badly. Remember that consumers can be fickle: people will tend to buy what they want and leave what they don't. It is much easier to swim with the tide than against it. If you want to make your sales team's job an easier one, find out what the public wants and get them to sell that - rather than trying to sell simply what you are currently producing.

3
DEVELOP REPEAT BUSINESS

IT'S HARD to sell to customers once, so work out how to create a back catalogue of products or ways to get your customers returning regularly.

Do you know the hardest person to sell to? It is somebody who doesn't know who you are, doesn't know anything about you, and essentially doesn't trust you. That is a difficult person to sell to.

Imagine you were thinking of buying a second-hand car and saw in a newspaper classifieds the model that you were looking for but at a surprisingly low price. You went round to the house where it was on sale and it turned out that that person was an old friend of yours. Before you looked at the car, he spent half an hour catching up on old times and remembering people you used to know. By the time it came to looking at the car, assuming it was in reasonable condition, you would almost certainly buy it from them.

If however, it was somebody you'd never met, you would look at the car much more carefully. You'd be very suspicious of this stranger selling the car at below-market price.

If we know and trust somebody, we are much more likely to buy from them.

It is exactly the same with your business. If a customer has bought from you several times in the past, they are much more likely to buy from you again as long as they had a good experience. This applies to any type of organisation because people can either repeat purchase for themselves, or in some situations where a one-off purchase is all that is required (perhaps a wedding dress shop) they can refer friends and family to that business.

When our family first visited Legoland near Windsor, I was surprised at the message that hit me almost as soon as we walked into the park. While there were plenty of posters promoting gift shops, cafes and lunches, the most dominant message was urging people to upgrade to an annual pass. At that time, the message that they were putting forward explained that an annual pass worked out cheaper than buying even a second ticket in the next 12 months. Because our two boys were the right sort of age for Legoland, we decided to upgrade and ended up coming back twice within the next 12 month period.

The clever thing that Legoland did was to make us visit more than once within that time period. Normally, because of the distance we had to travel to get there, we wouldn't have visited again for at least another year. By making the offer, they had encouraged us to pay more visits to the park than we would normally have done. Why? Because we had experienced it, enjoyed the visit, and – perhaps under some pressure from children – decided it was a good idea to come again. The message of upgrading to an annual pass was not widely advertised outside the park, but was advertised a lot inside the park to existing customers who are much more likely to upgrade, having experienced the event already for themselves.

The question is: where does the real profit lie in places like Legoland? In the repeat business from existing customer spending money in gift shops, restaurants and on merchandise.

So the next time you introduce a new product to your range, or perhaps when you have a storeroom of old stock, remember that the people most likely to buy from you are those who have bought from you in the past. While you should never give up on winning new business (and it is essential that any company has new people walking through your door for the first time) the people most likely to actually buy from you are old customers. Don't neglect them. Don't stop writing to them. Never upset them by ignoring them with offers only reserved for shiny new or potential customers, because their loyalty should be rewarded.

If you are in a business where customers tend to buy from you only once, it is likely worth looking at your entire business model. What other products or services can you develop? Can you do affiliate deals with non-competitor companies where you can sell their products in addition to your own? If you have a one-product sale that people only need once, I would ask questions about how successful your business will be in the long term because it depends so heavily on winning new business all the time.

By the way, if you ever doubt how profitable repeat business is, just think about the cigarette industry. How profitable would it not be if people who smoked only ever bought one packet of cigarettes? The tobacco industry's research shows that the average smoker will spend £87,000 over their shortened lifetime at today's prices.

4

CREATE NICHE PRODUCTS FOR NICHE AREAS

LET ME ASK you a ridiculous question. Can you make a hole in a wall using only light? You might be surprised to know that the answer is yes, but this is not a normal light. It is only when the light is focused into a laser beam that it will enable you to punch a hole in the wall. This idea illuminates the principle of marketing to niche areas.

Generally accepted wisdom would be in agreement with the statement that 'anybody can be a customer'. Essentially the wider the customer base, the more chance you give your business. I often hear companies say something along these lines: "We don't have any particular sector that we operate in because anybody can buy our product." Through years of attending networking groups and witnessing the result of direct mail campaigns, I can tell you that, perhaps surprisingly, as widely accepted as this idea is, in fact the opposite is the case.

If you are able to focus your marketing activities on one very specific niche area that you know has a real need for your product and you spell out the specific benefits of your product to businesses or people within that area, your marketing efforts will have a dramatically better effect than if you spray-market large areas.

The most effective place to start is to look at where your customers currently are (the sectors or geographical areas that they occupy) and then to create a series of different messages specific to each of those major – profitable – sectors. By doing this one thing, you will discover a dramatic improvement in your response rates.

The reason that this idea works so well is that you have now created a product that, as far as they are concerned, has been developed to specifically fit their needs. Previously it felt as though you were writing to them as part of the crowd and then they had to work out a couple of steps for themselves about how that product could be adapted for them. Now you're doing the thinking for them and this time you have actually created something for their sector, so they can instantly see how they or their company will benefit from what you're offering.

I have seen this used in so many different sectors and I know that it works in every case. Think about your own niche in the market and work out the pain that people in that sector are currently suffering to see how your product can help overcome that problem. Now market directly to them, emphasising the specifics rather than the general benefits your product has to offer.

5

DON'T AIM TO BE THE CHEAPEST, AIM TO BE THE BEST

DO YOU GET a sense of pride and satisfaction from the work you do? Is it important to you to do a great job that makes your customers happy? Do you look at some of the other companies in your market and shake your head and think 'What a bunch of cowboys and how dare they try to get away with that?'

If that's the case – and I would imagine that it is with most of the people reading this book – then you should not beat yourself up for being more expensive than some of your competitors. Whatever market you are in and however competitive it is, it is important to acknowledge that there will always be some businesses that are expensive and some that will try to undercut everything you do. While on the surface the cheap companies seem to do well (and if you have a sales force, you will often be told "We can't compete against them because of their prices") it is really not good business practice to be in the bottom quarter during a price war.

Even in tough times, people go for the best value rather than the cheapest. If I buy a pair of shoelaces for £1, they may last me two years. If I buy some for 20p, they may last me a week. Which offers the best value?

 What we obtain too cheap, we esteem too lightly; it is dearness only that gives everything its value."

—*Thomas Paine*

6

WATCH YOUR LANGUAGE: USE THE 'YOU' WORD, NOT THE 'WE' WORD

THE CLASSIC mistake when writing a company brochure, company letter or any other type of marketing material is to assume two things. First of all, that the material is about 'us' as a business. Secondly, that people are interested in our business and that is why they are reading the marketing material. These are both mistakes and most people make them in their marketing.

Let's examine the first one.

Your marketing material is not about you! Or at least it shouldn't be. Your marketing material is about how you help your customers. Write about how you can overcome problems that they are currently experiencing, how you can increase their profits, how you can generally make their lives better if they use your product. They don't really care much about when your company was formed or who works for the company, although a little bit of that towards the end of the brochure might be fine for establishing your credibility within the industry. The bulk of your brochure should be identifying problems that they have at the moment and then explaining how your company and the products your company offers can help them.

The second mistake is to assume is that people are interested in your company. Perhaps one day they will be if you deliver them remarkable results, but for the moment that's not the case. At the moment they are only interested in your company insofar as it can help solve a problem that they have.

Let's look at two very diverse examples: Slimfast and Amazon.com.

In the Slimfast TV and press commercials, do they talk about how the company was formed, who runs it or its projected turnover? Of course they don't. They talk about how it helps people to slim – fast. They talk about how their products help people to lose weight rapidly. They use appetising looking pictures of the product. They show before and after pictures of people who have used the product. And that's pretty much it. Everything in their advertising is focused on the result that the product will achieve for you. And in fact the same goes for any other successful diet product. It focuses on the clear benefits that the product delivers.

Amazon.com sell a huge volume of books (any many other items) online. For many people they are the first website to turn to when buying online, making it the second most visited site in the UK. By allowing people to enter the title of the book or the author's name or a particular genre, it makes it very easy to buy either a specific book or to browse through a wide selection of books on topics from marketing to curry and everything in between. Of course there are other sites, but Amazon delivers items quickly, has regular special offers and there are lots of other things that they do to make your buying experience pleasurable. I have bought items from Amazon for many years, but do I have the first idea about when the company was formed or who owns it or where the offices are or anything like that? No, I don't, and I don't think I'm really very interested in any of that. I trust it as a company and as a brand, but I'm interested in it only as far as it helps me buy books and other items in a convenient way.

Now that you understand people aren't interested in you or your business as much as the benefits your business delivers to them, you understand the biggest crime in most people's marketing. If you look at the majority of websites, brochures, direct mail letters and other documentation, you will usually see the word 'we' an enormous number of times – often opening paragraphs: 'we' do this, 'we' do that. When you look further into the paragraphs it's 'we' were established in... 'we' work with etc. The word 'we' appears too many times.

In order to make your text more engaging to potential customers, you need to have a major shift of focus in the text. Try to replace as many 'we' words with 'you' words. How do you do that? If a typical sentence reads: 'We are based in Wembley High Street where we have been since 1973', change it to a sentence along the lines of: 'If you travel to Wembley High Street on a regular basis, you might have noticed our shop located beside the post office. You might have walked past it dozens of times. Well now we are inviting you to join us next time you go past and claim a 10 per cent discount off any purchase'.

There's a distinct difference in tone between those two sentences. One is aloof, distant and focused on the business. The other is focussed on the customer and their experience.

7

WRITE TO PEOPLE OR COMPANIES YOU WOULD LIKE TO WORK WITH

MOST BUSINESSES will sit and wait until people find them. They cross their fingers and hope that people will cross the street. In fact, obvious as it may sound, the best way to attract the companies or individuals that you would like to work with is to decide exactly who they are. In my experience, the vast majority of business owners never do this.

Let's start with a business that deals with other businesses. By examining your existing invoices, records and customer base, it should be clear which types of businesses are the most profitable for you. Let's say that light bulb manufacturers represent a good portion of your business. You can see that they are good payers, but they seem to really need the service you provide and for some reason seem keen to recommend your business onto others. However, when you look at the total number of light bulb manufacturers you work with, you discover that you only currently work with 10 per cent of the market. Although you have never actively targeted the sector, through word-of-mouth and natural staff migration in this area, it appears to be quite successful for you.

Imagine you are a shopkeeper who sells shoes. You notice from your records that most of your customers come from the downtown area, with a majority close to the railway station. You also notice that a higher-than-average number of your customers come from certain villages. Finally you notice that school teachers appear to be the profession that uses your shop more than any other.

In both of the above cases, it would appear that there are distinct patterns emerging. Although you have never targeted specific sectors, it is clear that certain geographic, professional and business areas are interested in your products and service. It is worth pointing out at this juncture that most companies will not take the time to examine their database in this way. So the fact that you are doing it at all will set you ahead of the competition.

By simply purchasing data relevant to the sectors that are most interested in your products, or by targeting a leafleting campaign in those areas offering special incentives to come in and visit your business, you will find that you will generate a better-than-average response rate.

Rather than leave things to chance and treat all prospects as equal, it is far more cost-effective from every angle to target those people or businesses that are most likely to come to you with a concentrated effort. The conversion is money well spent.

BUILD UP A DATABASE OF THE BIG FISH THAT YOU WOULD LIKE TO WORK WITH

MY YOUNGEST son is a big Arsenal fan and it would be a dream come true for him were he ever to step out onto the pitch at the Emirates Stadium. At the moment, it would appear his chances are not very high, but it's good to have a clear ambition about what your ultimate 'success' in a particular area would look like.

What is your version of Arsenal for your business? Who are the ultimate companies that you'd love to work with? One way of defining them is by identifying sectors or parts of the country with specific companies, perhaps market leaders that would enhance your reputation by association. Alternatively you may opt for companies that are close to you so that you provide them with better service simply through their close proximity to you.

Your business might be in an industrial estate surrounded by dozens of other companies. A natural place to start might be to write to all of those companies and invite them to a free event that you are holding in your business. Taking the net wider, you may decide to write to the top 50 or 100 companies in your county. These companies may well be working with your competitors at the moment, but it is quite possible that they are unhappy with some aspects of the service that they are receiving. This is the beginning of a gradual process of building up a relationship with them.

Later in this book we will talk about gaining positive PR coverage from your business. We will also be talking about how to write successful direct mail letters. Remember this section when you are reading these later parts of the book. A great way to increase the perceived size of your business is to focus your activities on very specific businesses that you would choose to work with.

By drawing up a shortlist of target companies, you can focus more of your marketing activity on them. Keep in touch with them on a regular basis. Find out the names of the most important decision-makers within them. Invite them as guests to events you host or even that you are attending; send them special offers; send them press cuttings – in fact, send them anything relevant and interested on a regular (monthly) basis to keep your name in their mind. Soon, if you start calling them up, they won't think that you're a stranger.

If you've done your marketing right, they will recognise your name and certainly your company's name. Now that your first call isn't a cold call, it's far more likely to result in an appointment. In their mind, they will imagine you are a much larger business than you already are. It's a very simple approach, but for smaller businesses looking to work with larger organisations, it is a good and cost-effective way of improving your perception with your ideal customer.

ALASTAIR CAMPBELL

9
ATTEND REGULAR NETWORKING EVENTS

WHEN I SET up my business in 2003, I don't think I had ever attended a networking event. The idea of walking into a room full of strangers, going up to somebody I didn't know, shaking their hand and making small talk seemed absolutely terrifying. For many people, it is an idea that fills them with dread and trepidation.

The good news is that there are different networking events for every possible type of person. There are specific trade and industry events, there are events that are very informal and there are much more structured events where many people find it is easier to talk business – because that is what they are told to do. Each type of event has its own advantages and disadvantages, and it would be unfair to single out any particular structure of organisation for praise or blame. The truth is that to a large extent, networking is what you decide to make of it.

However, there are one or two different types or formats of event that I would suggest seem to work best for most businesses.

While you should always try to find out for yourself which specific organisation suits your requirements, you might find the following suggestions helpful.

Regular weekly meetings: If you have not discovered the world of early morning business networking meetings, you may be astonished how many of these types of events take place in a hotel near you on a regular basis. The BNI (Business Networks International) and B for B (Business for Breakfast) are two such organisations which offer weekly meetings with the twin purpose of passing new business and establishing links between potential suppliers in the local area.

You'll probably find many similar but smaller organisations that operate only in your region or area. I have been in a Leicester-based networking group called Working Breakfast since 2004. The format of our group is similar to many others, and should give you an indication of how such meetings work.

We meet each Wednesday at 7am. At 7.15 we get our breakfast and sit down at the table. At 7.30 the formal part of the meeting begins. The membership team members introduce themselves: they usually have an education spot where somebody explains an idea which has helped people's businesses (usually focused around better networking). Then everybody in the group – typically around 20 business owners – is given the opportunity to speak for 60 seconds. They ask other people within the group to refer specific business types on to them. This may be a particular company or it may be a particular product or service that they currently have on special offer.

Each week somebody is given the opportunity to do a 10-minute presentation. The group also encourages One-to-One meetings outside of the main meeting where members can get to know each other's business better.

The group I belong to runs on a not-for-profit basis. That means that the money we pay into the group stays within the group and is used to promote each other's services, pay for trips to local restaurants, and once a year we go on an annual training conference event. The overall effect is that as business owners we do what we can to help one another. Over time it has proved a very successful formula.

At the end of each meeting, leads are passed around the room with contact details of potential businesses written on them. This means that members can leave the room at 8.30 starting their new working day with contacts for potential new business. Over the past six months, I have received around 100 new business leads from the group which are worth to me around £500 each. Not all will actually turn into business, but enough of them have to pay for my £250 membership fee many, many times over.

It's also worth pointing out that it can be a great way of building suppliers and friends when you are starting up in business.

This regular structured business networking event is not for everyone. It requires the discipline of regular attendance, a certain amount of altruism because we look out for and try to help other business owners. Some people would find this level of commitment too much and would rather not invest the time and effort in order to make such networking activity a success.

An alternative approach can be found in organisations such as The Business Club, the Federation of Small Business (FSB) or similar less frequent and less structured networking events.

Typically these are evening events running between 7pm and 9pm. The event begins with some open networking and then members are asked to sit down. There is usually the opportunity to pitch their business to other people at the table or the whole room. These events often have an educational speaker who talks on a relevant business topic for between 20 minutes and an hour. There is no formal structure or imperative to pass on business at such events, but members are encouraged to help other members. These types of events take place all over the country and can have as many as 100 people in the room working with one another.

If you are new to networking, three simple rules should stand you in good stead.

Firstly, if you are going up to a group of strangers, it is easier to join a group with an odd number of participants than an even number. So for example going up to one person standing on their own group or a group of three or five is likely to be more successful than going up to groups of two, four or six.

Secondly, don't try to sell on the night. By all means engage in conversation and talk about what your business does, but it is far better to ask questions, listen, and then ensure you have the contact details of the other person than to bore them to death telling them everything about your business and trying to close a sale on the spot. It is rude and won't make you any friends.

Thirdly, remember that with so many people coming and going at these events, it is often difficult to stand out from the crowd. If you're doing a 60-second presentation, can you make it visual? If you have something to say to people, can you make it memorable? Is there something about your product or service that you can give them as a sample? As Oscar Wilde said, the only thing worse than being talked about is not being talked about. Most people blend into the background, so think of a way you can stand out from the mass.

For more detailed advice on Networking visit www.kintish.co.uk for free tips and advice. It's a company run by Will Kintish who specialises in training people on how to grow their business through networking.

> " More business decisions occur over lunch and dinner than at any other time, yet no MBA courses are given on the subject."
>
> —Peter Drucker

10
GO TO WHERE YOUR CUSTOMERS GO

WHICH TRADE events do your customers (not your competitors) go to? If you are an accountant, it is easy to go to events with lots of other accountants. If you're a plumber, the same holds true, as it does for most trades and professions. But it is equally easy to find events with lots of customers. Potential customers can often be found in shoals; they tend to congregate at different types of events. For example, to an accountant, a fertile source of new business could be events aimed at start-up businesses. Every business needs an accountant from its early days, and if you offer a special package for start-up businesses and can catch them at a key formative stage, it could prove to be very fruitful for you.

If you have particular business areas that you like working with, think about what type of events – trade shows, exhibitions or seminars – these people are likely to attend and make a note of seeking them out or even sponsoring such events. Networking doesn't have to involve broad and general audiences, nor does it have to involve your direct competitors. It can be about going straight to the source of your potential customers and catching them while they are in the mood to spend money with either you or your competitors.

> **They may forget what you said, but they will never forget how you made them feel."**
>
> —Carl W Buechner

11
DEVELOP THE PHILOSOPHY OF 'NEXT'

NOBODY IN business has it easy all the time. Many business owners have failed, become bankrupt or come very close to throwing in the towel. The difference between a successful entrepreneur and an unsuccessful one is often down to a single event and a difference in attitude.

One of the best business philosophies I have ever heard is from the great direct marketing expert Ted Nicolas. He talks about the philosophy of next, and I would like to share his idea with you here. Ted says that rather than let things get to you when they go wrong, you should look at the project and seek out which parts of it worked well. Even if it is a project which has ended in disaster, some things about it will have been a success.

Look at the elements that did not work – why did they go wrong? Did you not give yourself enough time? Was one element of the project planning particularly poor? How much better could you have made it if you were able to redo it? You can often learn as much from a failure as you can from a success. Once you have taken these lessons on board, you are now in a position to apply what you learned to your next project.

Ted Nicholas is a world-famous marketer with an amazing number of successful projects behind him, but he would be the first to admit that not everything he has tried has worked. One of the reasons that he has become so successful is his willingness to spend time looking at what didn't work and, when necessary, cutting his losses, moving on to the next project and taking those lessons with him.

By constantly examining what we have done right and what we have done wrong, we can rapidly build our businesses by learning from mistakes and focusing on successes. It is clear that when a project is doomed to failure and is only going to cost you time and effort, you need to act quickly and cut your losses. Admit it when you have made a mistake and learn from the experience. And move on to the next project.

Rather than give up and blame yourself or other people for what might have been, it is best to accept the truth, roll up your sleeves and decide that next time things will be different. We can all learn from the mistakes of ourselves and others. But rather than take it to heart and give up, it is better to say 'next' and quickly move on.

12

EVERYBODY CONNECTED WITH YOUR BUSINESS IS INVOLVED IN MARKETING IT

HOW MANY people are connected with your company? It may just be you, or you may have hundreds of people who work in different capacities. You may also have a number of suppliers, from a bank manager to a part-time bookkeeper.

While you may have some people whose specific responsibility is sales and marketing, the truth is that everybody in your organisation or closely linked to it is actually involved in the sales and marketing.

Think how many people we all know. On the business networking site LinkedIn, if you are connected to 500 people, the actual number of connections including third parties is actually likely to be more than four million.

The interesting thing of course is that we are only connected to a fraction of the people we know on LinkedIn. So imagine how many people could potentially hear about your business in a good light if everybody within the organisation and associated people had good things to say about it.

We may take time and effort in explaining to our sales staff the new product ranges and the new advantages of using our products and services, but how much time do we take to educate other people in the organisation? This might not be done on a formal basis, but there is a host of other subtle ways, such as having products on display, running strategically placed information videos, circulating regular customer and internal newsletters, that you can spread the message about what you're hoping to achieve in the business. Using methods like these, you can educate a great deal of your new extended sales and marketing team who could potentially spread the word about what you do.

So don't think of your sales force as your only sales team. You never know who is going to come into contact with somebody who knows your organisation and ask questions like 'What do you do?' or 'Who do you work for?' or 'Do you know a company that...' If you're able to take the time to educate and explain the advantages of what you do to everybody from suppliers to part-time staff, you would be surprised how many additional enquiries you may receive over time.

13

SALESMANSHIP IS THE TRANSFER OF ENTHUSIASM TO ANOTHER PERSON

IT IS A COMMON misconception that people do not like being sold to. In fact, when it is done well, people love being sold to. What we object to is when people will try and sell us things that we don't want and we don't need – and it's perfectly clear they are not listening to what we say.

Have you ever been into a garage to look for a car? I remember one occasion when I was in the market for a new car. I was pleased when a salesperson came up to me because I had some specific questions I wanted answered. I asked three questions; he didn't know the answer to any of them and didn't even offer to give me an answer. Instead he tried to sell me a car.

I made it quite clear that I was not interested in the particular model he was trying to sell me, however he kept on trying to sell it to me – clearly a waste of time for both of us.

He wasn't going to persuade me to buy a car that I didn't have any interest in, so why was he wasting his breath? What made things considerably worse was that he seemed particularly bored with his job. A couple of times he stopped to tell me about what a bunch of idiots the management were and the problems that he had been experiencing. This might have got him some sympathy, if I had not agreed with what they were saying about him.

I walked out of the showroom knowing perfectly well that I would be added to his list of things to complain about that day. If only he had listened to me, I was giving him clear buying signals for a completely different car to the one he was trying to sell me. But because I disliked him and was not particularly impressed by either his level of understanding or his attitude, I certainly had no intention of giving him my business.

Contrast that with a different type of salesperson: somebody who understands their products and is clearly enthusiastic about the benefits that they can offer. Somebody who wants to serve the customer in whichever way they can. Would you buy from that person? Of course you would. We'd all be happy to buy something if it meets our needs and our price expectations, and of course we have spoken to somebody who does his or her best to understand what we require and how the product will benefit us.

If this quest for knowledge about us and our needs is matched by the salesperson's enthusiasm for the product, then we have every likelihood of completing the purchase. Sadly not many people show a lot of enthusiasm, so the good news is that if you are one of the people who does, the chances are you will sell, and become very successful at it.

14
FIND THE GAPS

LOOK FOR additional products and services that you can offer to your existing clients. If you already have a range of products that are useful to your customers, it can be easy to think that this is all they will want to buy from you. You know your place in the market and you supply to people who appreciate what you do.

While there will always be examples of companies that come unstuck after they diversify, there is no harm in exploring product or brand extensions in order to grow your market share.

Cadbury's for example has long been known for its chocolate bars. But from the latter part of the 1990s and onwards, it diversified into a very successful range of ice creams. The problem for Cadbury's was that while in Britain chocolate sales were strong for much of the year, sales fell in the summer months. By offering a range of branded Cadbury's ice creams during the hot summer months, the company was able to offset the low volume of chocolate sales and of course keep people aware of the Cadbury's brand and unique chocolate flavour. In fact, if you go to the freezer cabinet now, you will notice that more than half of ice cream products are linked to confectionery you could find all year round. Mars, Twix and Bounty ice cream are all now found in the freezer cabinet. All are items that 20 years ago you would have found only in the newsagents or supermarket shelf.

Coca-Cola and other soft drinks no longer content themselves with a single flavour of the product. In order to cater to different markets and different segments, they have produced a wide range of variations. Traditional Coke with its distinctive red can is still a popular seller, but now Diet Coke, Coca-Cola Zero and Cherry Coke, along with many other variations, are also found on the supermarket shelves. Each type caters for, but does not exclusively appeal to, a different market sector. For example, Diet Coke is strongly marketed toward a young female audience, while Coca-Cola Zero targets a young male audience.

By extending the original Coca-Cola brand into these different directions, the manufacturer had been able to maintain a strong hold of the market while offering slightly different products to different areas and creating a special brand around each one.

I appreciate that you and I are not Coca-Cola with its many hundreds of millions of dollars to spend each year on advertising and marketing, but we can learn a great deal from this market segmentation and introduction of new products.

If you are already offering a product which appeals successfully to truck drivers, for example, what other items do you currently not sell the truck drivers but on a regular basis they need to buy? Are there other items that you could either manufacturer or begin stocking and reselling that would appeal to that audience?

The point is that they are already coming to you to buy certain items, making them a ready-built market.

Direct Line is an insurance company. When it originally launched, Direct Line sold only car insurance. This was in the 1980s but nowadays it sells everything from health insurance to pet insurance pet to house insurance for landlords. By originally creating demand for one product, it was then able to look at the needs of its existing customers and ask the question: 'What else can we sell this group?' Product by product, it was able to offer other types of insurance to its existing customers and ultimately was able to expand into new areas which it didn't cover. By carefully analysing the enquiries which came in and looking at the other insurance products which were available, it steadily built its customer base and its product range.

The easiest way to introduce new products is to look at your existing customer base and then ask the question: 'If they are currently buying this from us, what else might they be interested in buying?' Some simple market research into what they might be interested in and you could start launching new product extensions which could rapidly grow your business.

15

TAKE TIME TO EXPLAIN TO YOUR TEAM WHAT YOU WANT FROM THEM AND WHERE YOU ARE GOING

WHAT IS THE difference between goal-setting and targets? My definition is quite simple. Goal-setting is working out what you want to achieve and how to do it by setting dates and timelines, and then on an ongoing basis enthusiastically going about creating a course that you have decided on because it is important to you. Targets are something altogether different. Targets are imposed by either your boss, central government or some other external force which claims to know better than you what you should be doing in your job. A constant irritation of teachers is that they are being told by central government that children in the class should be performing at a specific level when often the teacher will know perfectly well what the child is capable of despite the average figures from the Department of the Education showing something entirely different.

One of the best ways to get your staff on board is to sit down and explain to them what your plans are for the business and ask them for their opinions and ultimately for their buy-in. Taking them through the process step by step, explaining what you're hoping to do with the company over the longer term, the different markets you are aiming for, why it's so important to retain customers, what plans you have to win new customers etc. All too many staff feel they're being treated like mushrooms – kept in the dark and covered in manure.

If you think about it, it is only logical that your staff will respond positively to your plans for the business. They want to make sure that their employment is secure and that they are working for a company with a good future. When staff get disgruntled, it is usually because either they don't know what's going on or they worry that the company is not doing well. If you feel confident that they can see the big vision for the company for which they work and – just as importantly – feel that they can significantly contribute towards the outcome, they are far more likely to be engaged on a day-to-day basis. We all enjoy having meaning to our work.

There is a story that illustrates this point well.

A building inspector in mediaeval France is walking along outside a construction site. In front of him, three men are working. He notices that they are doing the same job but at dramatically different rates. He approaches the first man who is working at the slowest pace and asks him what he's doing.

"I'm hauling stones from one pile to another," he replies. It's backbreaking work, he adds, the sun is hot and it feels like a never-ending task.

The inspector approaches the second man who appears to be working faster and asks him the same question. "I'm working on a project," he says. His task is taking stones from one area to another. The pay is reasonable and his prospects are okay and he is meeting the targets that have been set for him and so the chances of keeping his job are good.

Then the Inspector approaches the third man who appears to be doing the work of the other two men and perhaps more. The inspector struggles to interrupt him because he is working so enthusiastically.

"Can you tell me what you are doing?" he asks.

"I'm building the largest cathedral in Europe," he says. "It is an extraordinary work of engineering and will be here hundreds of years after I am no longer on this earth. I am honoured and privileged to be part of such an incredible project."

Three people carrying out the same job, but with very different results. Clearly the first man has no sense of what he is doing and is working with minimum effort to get by. The second man knows what he has to do, is doing it to keep his job and is focused on targets that he is meeting. The third man is inspired by the whole project and is doing the best he can because it is more than money for him – it is a mission.

All three are doing the same job, the same work, but their mental attitudes toward it are totally different. You could say that this apocryphal story illustrates how different personality types react to work, but I would think that perhaps they were working for three different divisions and had three different bosses who each took a different approach to managing their staff.

The chances are you have a strong vision for your business and you have a passion to make that business grow. If you do, share it with your staff and explain to them what you're trying to achieve with their help. If you get them on board, the journey will be a lot better for all of you. If you have staff all working for different reasons and pulling in different directions, it's very difficult to move forward.

> " Leadership is not about creating followers only. It's about creating other leaders. I'm at my finest as a leader when I have created an organisation full of individuals who can exercise leadership in support of the common goals and objectives that we share."
>
> —Nancy Greer

ALASTAIR CAMPBELL

16

CAN A SUCCESSFUL PRODUCT BE TRANSFERRED INTO A PARALLEL MARKET?

DO YOU CURRENTLY operate successfully in one market? If so, one way of growing your business could be to offer other products to market, as we have discussed earlier. However an alternative way to achieve growth is to look at parallel markets with certain similarities.

I worked for a telecoms company which very successfully marketed a phone system to GPs' surgeries. The result was that over time they had more than 25 per cent of all GPs' surgeries using the telephone equipment. It was an impressive share of the market, but at the end of the day, it was one market. At that rate, in a few years the company would have as much of the market as it could ever have. While part of its model was based on additional sales to the customers, it was clear that growth couldn't continue forever.

The answer for growth as far as the company was concerned was to continue looking after customers in that sector but to look at other sectors which had similar problems. In the telecoms company's case, after some research it made sense to expand into the dental market. Dentists share many of the problems and advantages that GPs have and so the company's experience in one sector was able to be transferred over into a second sector.

If you are currently successful in one area, then as a general rule you can succeed in a second provided they share similar problems to your original sector. By launching an almost identical product in a second sector, you have a good chance of success. Similarly, if you are already successful in one sector, if you have a good reputation and good relations with your existing customers, you could launch a second product in your original sector.

By making use of either your product expertise, or your sector expertise, you can expand into the market much further than you currently are and continue to do so year after year.

One small word of warning. I wouldn't recommend expanding into a different sector, with a different product to the one you're already successful with. This would probably be biting off more than you can chew. Better to stick with either the sector you know or the product you know in order to maximise chances of success.

ALASTAIR CAMPBELL

17

SEND OUT PRESS RELEASES REGULARLY

OFTEN WHEN I'm running my seminars, I will ask an audience at some point if they have sent out a press release so far this year. Given that these are generally small business owners, who have been in business for over a decade on average, how many people do you think raise their hands? It is a very rarely more than 50 per cent that have ever sent out a news release. Typically around 20 per cent have sent one out in the previous 12 months

That's a shame, for the reason that every business will have done something over the course of a year which on some level is newsworthy.

The news release sent out to local, industry, trade or even national press has a chance of being picked up if it is well-written and targeted at the readers or listeners of that publication or programme. Writing a press release and distributing it needn't take more than half a day, so really there should be nothing stopping businesses from using this very simple and straightforward form of publicising themselves.

Here are five things to remember about news releases.

No 1. Think about the publication you are sending it to and their readership. If it is a local newspaper, then the angle for your news release must be for local residents. If this is a trade release, this must be the focus of your story. Whether the publication is interested in your news is always relative to its readership. A very technical medical piece may not be interesting to a local audience – but it could be a fascinating read for a specialist pharmaceutical readership. Always start with audience in mind to decide whether your story will be of interest.

No 2. What are the facts? A news release is not an advert. Think about the facts of the story. What has happened, who has it happened to, why is this relevant to the readership, what implications does it have, why is it important? A news release should always be based on fact – something that happened that you wish to communicate with a wider audience. There is no point in making stories up out of thin air. Perfectly legitimate stories would include a major new contract win, new staff being taken on, premises being expanded, a survey of your customers on the current economic conditions, an award nomination, the retirement of a long-standing member of staff. In all of these cases, something has happened to your business which may be of interest to readers of a particular newspaper and magazine.

No 3. You should observe the accepted form of a news release. With small variations, it should always begin with the date you send the release out and the words 'news release' at the top of the page. Underneath should usually be a short sentence which acts as your headline. The sentence sums up the main points of the story. Underneath this you will have around four to five paragraphs of text.

The first paragraph should normally be a summary of all the key points of the story, written in an interesting way. The second paragraph amplifies this first paragraph, perhaps including some additional facts. The third paragraph may include a quote from the managing director of the company or other people involved in the story. The final paragraphs often can contain more quotes, more facts, or more relevant information to the story.

The news release should end with the word 'ends' and beneath that you should include contact details, preferably for two or three people, including a landline and mobile telephone number. The landline and mobile number will not be included when the story is published, but that information is there should the news editor or reporter wish to contact you for further clarification of the story or, in the case of radio, in case they wish to interview on air about what you have written.

No 4. The style of writing for your news release is very important. As mentioned earlier, the reporter is looking for facts. If you story is interesting, and you provide them with facts, then you have a good chance of being included.

Too many people exaggerate the facts and use too many descriptions in the main body of their text. So, for example, a sentence should read: 'In 2009 the company turned over £2 million but in 2010 the figure was £3.7 million. The company attributes the rise largely to increased demand for solar energy within local authorities.' It should not read: 'The company had a fabulous year with profits virtually doubling overnight. The storming performance was due to brilliant management, excellent teamwork and lots of hard work from the team.' If you did want to include a sentence similar to the second one, it would always need to be attributed to somebody in authority within the organisation, such as the managing director, as a quote.

Remember, the main body of the news release should be about facts. Any emotional reactions to the news should always be contained between quotation marks and attributed to the appropriate member of staff — even if that's you!

No 5. You may have several different audiences that you wish to tell about your good news. You want to get the story into the national newspapers, trade magazines, as well as your local newspapers and radio stations. The reasons for getting into each channel will be different but the main reason of course is to generate additional publicity and business. It is possible to do this if you have a strong story, however it is always important to bear in mind the audiences for those different outlets.

Most news will have several angles, so your task is to select the angle best suited to the audience. In the local version of the release, you should almost certainly include the name of the town and village in the title so that the news editor can quickly see that it is a news story relevant to the area. Similarly, if you are contacting a trade title, it makes sense to emphasise the particular skill, profession or business in the title so that they can see it is relevant to their audience. National press is more difficult but essentially the more interesting and relevant, topical and exciting the story appears to be, the better its chances of being picked up. I would only send a story to the nationals if I thought it stood a reasonable chance of appearing because it was a strong story – you can assess what editors consider strong by studying what they print. Perhaps your story can be linked to another major national topic that is relevant at the moment. If so, then the chances of you story being picked up will certainly be increased.

While there is no point in sending out news releases just the sake of it, it is a good idea to get into the habit of thinking about what is happening in your business that could make a useful news release. If you can aim to send out a news release every two months or so, then you can start to steadily gain ongoing coverage in the media for your company.

> Put it before them briefly so they will read it, clearly so they will appreciate it, picturesquely so they will remember it and, above all, accurately so they will be guided by its light."
>
> –Joseph Pulitzer

18

SEND OUT ARTICLE PITCHES REGULARLY

IN MY EXPERIENCE, less than one in 20 companies send out article pitches to newspapers and magazines. However, this can be one of the most effective ways of having your name and your company seen as being experts in your particular field.

The precondition for sending out an article pitch is that you are able to write the article you suggest. Therefore it makes sense to send out an article pitch on subject areas which are both an area of your expertise and that will help grow your business.

Here is how the process works.

First you need to decide on an interesting angle that will appeal to news editors. The important word to remember is the word 'news'. They are not interested in hearing about your company or about a general point within your industry that is not currently topical. The best starting point is to look at either the trade news or general news at the moment and see where the angle could fit in. Anything from the newly elected leader of a political party, an environmental disaster, pending strikes, rising crime figures – all of these background subjects could make a relevant article pitch if your business is linked with them in some way.

A client of ours was involved in managing large scale projects – in his case often linked with IT. When the launch of Heathrow Terminal 5 turned into a bit of a disaster, we saw an opportunity to pitch an article idea on the idea of 'how to launch major new projects'. His recommendation was phased implementation - the opposite of the approach that BA had used in T5. The result was that many business magazines asked him to write an article on this topic.

If you wish to write your article, it does not have to be directly linked with what you do in your day-to-day business, however there does have to be a connection or a parallel with your activity. Start to look at general news stories and see them through the eye of your profession.

Decide on which publications you would ideally like to be seen in. Obviously these magazines should be read specifically by your clients or targets or by a more general audience which could include your clients. Make a note of the news editors and if possible start to read these magazines on a regular basis to see the types of articles they currently publish. When an idea comes to you that you think would make an appropriate article, do not write the whole article. Instead write down a two or three sentence summary of what it would be about, why you think it could be of interest and in an additional paragraph, why you think that you are qualified to write this article, such as your background experience in this area.

Send this package along with a snappy headline to the news editors or section editors of the relevant titles, suggesting that you could write this article in return for brief mention of your services and company at the end. If it is a good strong article idea, you might be surprised how many editors come back to you requested either more information or saying that they will run it subject to its suitability. They will also tell you how many words they require and when they require it (the deadline).

Do not under any circumstances submit the same article to rival publications. If two or more publications expressed interest in the article, it is quite acceptable to adapt and create different versions of the same idea to different publications. So for example one article may be 500 words, while another may request 1,500. Even if both asked for a 1,000-word article, you would rewrite your story to include different headlines, different examples, rephrase the conclusion etc so that no two publications run an article that is the same.

When an editor comes back to you and gives you a deadline, make sure you submit it by or before that date if at all possible. This will give them the opportunity to read the article and edit it if they require changes. It is always a good idea is to offer photographs or submit them alongside the article.

Be warned: editors may also reject your article if it doesn't meet their editorial standards.

The magazine will normally send you a copy of the issue in which your article has appeared. In addition, if you request it, they will often send you a PDF of your article which you can use on your website or print out and sent to relevant contacts, as a way of keeping in touch with them.

19

WHAT DOES YOUR COMPANY STAND FOR?

HAVE YOU created a brand for your business? Branding is not just for big businesses. Every company should have an essential message at its core for what it stands for. For example, the Ideal Marketing Company is about effective low-cost marketing solutions that help small business owners. We don't try to offer marketing solutions to large corporate and international organisations; we focus instead on owner-managed businesses which want assistance with creating new enquiries and new business with limited marketing resources. Everything we produce is focused on this audience.

So start off by thinking about who your audience is and how can you serve them better. Is there a metaphor for what you do, that your audience could identify with? What does your company stand for? What are your core values?

For one client of ours, it was clear that their out-of-town shopping centre was almost an antidote to city centre covered shopping malls. While the new city centre shopping experience was certainly convenient and popular with many elements of the population, some people preferred traditional shops, over a smaller site with more of a personal service. The image we created for this shopping village was focused around the phrase 'Shopping as it should be', and had a distinctly Victorian feel – which was echoed by the site itself. We positioned it as a very different shopping experience from the crowded busy city centre that people had become used to.

Another client offers training services which help people think in a different way. For them, we created a simple visual which showed a valley / mountain scene. Through the middle of the picture was a path which split, going in 2 directions. One way led to the summit, the other meandered along to the valley floor. The proposition was simple: if you had to choose whether you reached the summit of stayed in the shadows, which route would you choose? Given that their programme was about peak performance, it was a simple metaphor that helped to explain the complex message.

By creating a brand for your business, you not only increase the value of your company, you can create a vision for the customer so they can see more clearly what it is you stand for, how you can help them and what makes you stand out from the competition.

ALASTAIR CAMPBELL

20
IMPROVE YOUR CUSTOMERS' PERCEPTION OF YOU VIA SPONSORSHIP OF THE RIGHT EVENT

IF YOU ARE clear about what your company stands for and who your target audience is, sponsorship of the right event can be a great way to appeal to them.

Sponsorship can also be very useful if you want to slightly alter the perception of your business. For example, if your product is associated with good health, but you want to give it a closer association to activities and sport, then sponsoring an athletic event might make sense.

The most important rule regarding sponsorship is that there should be a definite link between what you do and the event concerned. This link can be directly through associating the product with the event, or it may be more indirect – such as a local company sponsoring a local football team in order to influence local councillors or local parents.

The biggest question mark regarding sponsorship is whether it is good value for money and therefore worthwhile undertaking. By putting your name on the shirt of a team or the banner for an event, you link yourself very closely with it. Is the event something you want to be closely associated with?

Think about some of the sponsors of the London Marathon. Gillette, Mars and NutraSweet are all quite different companies but all wish to have different associations with the event. Gillette at the time was very keen to promote an active lifestyle and general manliness associated with its brand. NutraSweet with linking its brand to help and the ability to lose weight, while Mars had an implied energy boost associated through sponsorship. Each company saw different opportunities to be linked to a major prestigious sporting event watched the world over.

Many smaller local companies are more than happy to sponsor local children's football or rugby team. If your child plays in the team, or you just want to put something back into the community, this is of course a commendable and perfectly acceptable way of spending your money. However, if you're looking to get genuine value from your sponsorship, you may wish to look around at different types of sporting events to see whether one could be associated with your business. For example if you were a double glazing company, could you use the sponsorship in your advertising, perhaps promoting the fact that your windows are more resistant to damage than single glazed windows? By creating advertising messages surrounding the sponsorship, you get far better value for money from the sponsorship, and if the sponsored event is appropriate to your business, it can generate enquiries and also create a stronger branding associated with your company.

ALASTAIR CAMPBELL

21

ALWAYS ASK WHERE PEOPLE HEARD ABOUT YOUR COMPANY WHEN THEY FIRST ENQUIRE

WHEN TIMES are good, the phones are ringing and the e-mails are flying in filled with enquiries – who needs to ask where a new customer heard about you? Well actually you do. It is just as important to enquire during the good times as the difficult times.

When I speak to potential new clients, one of the questions I ask is how they generate enquiries at the moment? While a percentage of people will usually explain that they get recommended by their existing customers (which is a good thing, of course) it is surprising how few people know which elements of their current advertising and marketing mix work for them. They talk about adverts in local papers, in local free sheets, sponsoring of events, perhaps local radio advertising or Yellow Pages adverts. However they are seldom able to point to a particular campaign as a success.

Given that most of the companies I speak to are already reasonably successful, it would be a fair presumption to make that something they are currently doing in advertising and marketing already is working for them. However, most companies don't know what advertising works and what advertising does not.

The simplest way of getting at least a good indication is setting in place a very strict rule to ask everybody who enquires how they found out about your business.

Not everyone will tell you, and perhaps not everyone will know, but it will give you a good indication of what may be working and, equally important, what may not be working for you.

If you advertise in a variety of places at one time, the results may not be 100 per cent certain, but it does give you a strong indication about which advertising message the prospect saw that persuaded them to come to you. What I mean by this is that if you have a poster displayed in the town, are running a radio campaign, have recently leafleted an area, and also ran a newspaper advert, your name and message is hopefully being seen by people several times. In reality it's the combination of these messages that combine to make people contact you. It is their increased familiarity with what you do that has made them take action. If asked, they may say they found you through Google, but it was the various messages in various media that made them search out your website before buying online.

However, by asking each and every time somebody makes their first enquiry where they heard about you, you can build up at least a reasonable picture which gives a good idea of what advertising is working for you and what is not.

Why does this matter? It matters for two very important reasons. If you are spending your money equally with different publications, yet one publication consistently brings in twice as many enquiries per pound spent as the other publications, does it make sense to spend more money with the successful publication and less money with the unsuccessful publication? The result of following this strategy should be even more enquiries for the same amount of money spent. In other words, it means that you're able to balance your marketing so that the areas which generate the most enquiries get more money spent on them while those that generate fewer enquiries either get less money spent on them or you stop spending on them altogether.

The second important reason it matters is if you decide you need to cut your marketing spend. In a general downturn, or perhaps just when you have some cash flow issues, you may decide to reduce the amount of money spent on marketing. If you don't know which of your marketing outlays is generating the enquiries, how would you know which areas to cut? By monitoring what you're currently doing, you take the guesswork out of the picture. The problem with guessing is that we can easily allow false perceptions to get in the way. Your personal preference for a particular type of advertising or a particular publication can mask the true picture. By cutting a very successful advertising campaign without realising it, we can seriously affect new business opportunities coming our way.

The simplest way around this is to devise a form for anybody answering the phone to act as a prompt to asking a few simple questions about how you customer found out about the company. Filled in, those forms become your raw survey data. That way you can start toward success in your marketing by spending more on what works and less on what doesn't.

22

CREATE A NEWSLETTER FOR CUSTOMERS AND PROSPECTS

THE BIGGEST reason why customers fail to remain loyal to you is not because of price or bad service; it is because of perceived indifference. That means that your competitors show more interest than you do. If you think about it, you can see how easily this can happen.

We all get very excited about the idea of winning new business. Entrepreneurs in particular are on the whole much more interested in winning new customers than maintaining existing ones. As result, too much of the marketing budget is spent on acquiring customers rather than maintaining customers.

Have a look at your current marketing budget and see how much of it is spent on acquiring new business rather than keeping existing customers happy. You might be surprised just what a gulf there is between two.

One of the easiest ways of showing your existing customers that you haven't forgotten about them is to begin a regular company newsletter. This doesn't have to be an expensive affair, it could be a simple as a regular e-mail updates to customers about new products and events and services that you offer.

I would also suggest that your newsletter is in keeping with all your other marketing activities. So, for example, if you are a Rolls-Royce franchise selling only brand-new Rolls-Royces to people earning more than £100,000 a year, it would make sense to produce an attractive glossy newsletter that is sent by post. If, however, you sell ink cartridges at knockdown prices, then a price-led e-mail newsletter is perfectly sufficient. The point is that you do something on a regular basis that is appropriate to the type of material your customer has got used to from you.

By doing this you are showing your customers that you haven't forgotten about them, and that you are interested in continuing to do business with them. You are making it easy for them to carry on buying from you. By featuring special promotional prices previews and other incentives that are for existing customers, you are sending a clear message that you value old customers every bit as much as you value new business.

23

THINK 'HOW CAN I HELP' RATHER THAN 'HOW CAN I SELL'

THERE ARE times when it is best to offer advice not to buy your product. And that, in the long term, can be the best bit of sales advice there is.

Hard to believe? It is absolutely true. People will respect you if you start to think about how you can help them, rather than how you can sell to them

Let's look at a recent example. A company came to me through recommendation and asked me about a product they were thinking of launching. We spent 20 minutes or so looking at their background and what they were thinking of doing. We looked through their potential market and the timescales involved. I then asked them about budget. They were thinking of spending in the region of £200,000 a month on TV and radio advertising.

Up until that point, I felt that I could help, but as soon as they said this, it was clear to me that they should be speaking to a much larger marketing company than mine. They would be spending more in a single month that most of my clients' annual marketing spend. And while in the past I have worked at large advertising agencies which dealt with clients who spent in excess of £10 million a year, this was no longer my area of expertise. So I suggested an advertising agency based near them which was more suited to handling their requirements.

Another example at the other end of the scale was a start-up business that asked me for advice and ideas on the best way to launch their new product aimed at young mothers. I happily gave them my free one-hour consultation. At the end, they asked me what I charged for marketing advice, and I told them the best thing they could do in the current situation was to read my book, *The Marketing Launchpad*, and perhaps attend one of my seminars. For the limited resources that they had and what they were hoping to do, I didn't think it was right for them to use my consultancy services. But an unexpected result was that they recommended several friends and family members to use my services over subsequent months.

The point is this: while it is always tempting to go for the successful close in the short term, you should always think about the long-term benefits to the customer. If you can honestly say with hand on heart that you think the best thing for the customer to do right now is to use your services, then by all means try to close the sale. However, if you think that the best thing for them to do is either to buy nothing or to use a much cheaper (and perhaps inferior to some people but acceptable to what they want) alternative, then that is the advice you should give them. And explain to them that when they are ready to upgrade to a larger model or to spend a bit more money or they take on more staff, that would be the time to come back to you.

24

LEARN FROM YOUR COMPETITORS

LOOK AT WHAT your competitors are doing. Where are they advertising, what does their website look like, what is their message?

I had the great honour of working with Sir Eric Peacock a few years ago when he chaired an event that I spoke at. When I meet successful business owners, I always ask them if they have one piece of advice that they would pass on to people thinking of setting up in business, or some general business advice that they have found beneficial over the years.

Some people will give you several ideas, some people will hedge their bets and say something like "it depends," but Sir Eric replied almost instantly. He looked at me straight in the eye and said, "Steal with pride."

I guess I looked a little surprised. "Steal with pride?" I said.

"Yes," he said, "look at what your competitors are doing. Look at what other successful companies in different sectors are doing and adapt it for your own business. If you are thinking of launching a business in one sector and the market leader is doing certain things you like, and the number two in the sector is doing certain things you like, take the elements you think work best and adapt them for your business."

It's a very simple point, but one that is well made. Look at advertising, marketing, direct mail, websites, posters – anything you like. Which ones do you like? Which ones have been profitable? Depending on the sector you are in, it could be that they build trust. It could be that they stop you in your tracks with a surprising image. It could be that there's a 24-hour telephone number. It could be that the website they use captures your e-mail address before giving you the information.

Whatever it is, look at successful companies, see what they're doing well, read the biographies of successful people and learn what they do on a day-to-day basis and 'steal' the idea.

Now when I say steal, I don't mean photocopy someone's sales letter and use it verbatim or anything quite so blatant. That really is stealing and against the law! What I mean is learn from what successful people do, adapt it for your own use and use it with pride. Think of it as standing on the shoulders of giants.

25

KEEP IN REGULAR CONTACT WITH YOUR EXISTING CUSTOMERS

IF YOU ARE a small company, the chances are that there are some massive companies – perhaps international ones – out there who could probably beat you on price most of the time. If you are a professional services company, such as an accountant or lawyer or a marketing consultancy, there are probably 100 other companies which are interested in your clients and who will be bumping into them at networking events or writing to them to try and take their business away from you.

The reason that your customers stay with your business is probably because of the personal relationship that you have built up with them. At some point, it was your charm or expertise that made them want to work with your company.

The risk is that, over time as you have become busier, you may have started to take them for granted; you don't speak to them as often as you used to.

We talked earlier about perceived indifference and how using newsletters is one way of overcoming it. If you are a smaller company, you can go one better. If you have 30 or fewer regular customers, I would recommend you set a new company policy that you get on the phone and speak to a customer at least once a day. You may already have a certain number of client meetings and other ways of keeping in touch, but to simply pick up the phone, call a customer and give them an idea or some type of advice or a suggestion or an update will almost certainly ensure that they remain a customer for longer.

Why? Because most people don't do this; most people allow their customers to drift away.

By making it your company policy that you keep in touch with your customers by phone, not by e-mail alone, you start to build or continue to build a much stronger relationship. It allows them to feel that they could pick up the phone and call you if they have a problem.

If you are a larger organisation, perhaps you could get some rota drawn up so that a team of people keep in touch with customers and between you, you make sure that all the customers are spoken to least once a month.

Whether large or small, I would recommend strongly that you have some system in place to ensure that you speak to customers on a regular basis to make them feel wanted, welcome and able to complain should they need to.

26

CREATE A 'STICKY' MESSAGE TO MAKE IT EASIER FOR YOUR CUSTOMERS TO TELL PEOPLE ABOUT YOU

THERE ARE literally dozens of reasons why advertising fails, from not determining the market to creating a message that is too complex for people to understand. But one reason why advertising succeeds and remains in people's minds for longer is that the campaign has a 'sticky' element to it.

'Sticky' simply means that there is something so striking and memorable about the campaign that it not only sticks in your memory after you have seen it, it is a message that can easily be passed on to other people.

The Meerkats in ComparetheMarket.com's campaign, the Honey Monster in Sugar Puffs, or Carlsberg Lager's 'Probably the best' message all have a central idea that's easy to talk about. Some use a simple benefit so that when people ask what the company does, you're able to repeat it almost without thinking. Or it may be a particularly memorable image or demonstration in the advert that you are able to communicate to other people.

Cadbury's is one famous British company that has used the

idea of creating a 'sticky' message over the years and has created a number of stand-out sticky messages.

The first is the image of a glass and a half of milk in every bar. For many years, the company used a device with an animation showing two glasses being poured into chocolate. Over time, this was turned into a simple animation in purple and white (Cadbury's colours). This memorable image not only created a lovely creamy sense about the bar of chocolate, it also persuaded many mothers that it wasn't such a bad thing for the kids to eat chocolate after all, with all that 'milky goodness'.

The glass and the half is of course a totally meaningless statistic. How big is the glass for starters? How big is the bar? Which size bar has all that milk in it, etc. However, the phrase has been repeated so many times that we accept it as fact.

The image of a glass and a half is not only used on the TV campaigns, it is repeated on point of sale merchandise. It has now become a 'frame' for all the commercials. 'A glass and a half production' is how their commercials are introduced to make the audience aware of what is to follow.

In 1998, Cadbury's created an advert that was talked about in playgrounds, pubs and offices around the country. It was even responsible for getting a 1980's pop classic back into the charts. It was the advert that didn't even pretend to make sense – but boy, was it sticky! It featured a man in a gorilla suit drumming to a Phil Collins track, and once you saw it, you remembered it.

Sometimes creating something sticky cannot be guaranteed, and sometimes campaigns take on a life of their own. However, if you think about deliberately trying to create some element of your campaign, be it a visual image, a slogan or a jingle, that is designed to stick in people's heads, you dramatically increase the chances of the message not only being remembered, but also being passed on.

> "There is only one thing worse than being talked about – and that's not being talked about."
>
> –Oscar Wilde

ALASTAIR CAMPBELL

27
SPEND MONEY ON THINGS THAT MATTER

HOW CAN you tell when a company is in trouble? It is often when the company directors start buying themselves cars whose price is the equivalent to most of their staff's salary. Your business may be doing well, but that does not mean you need to start spending money for the sake of it.

If you have spare cash in the business, why not invest in training for your staff or in marketing for your products to generate more money for expansion? The worst thing you can spend your money on is flash new offices, flash new cars, or flash new suits. It sends out the wrong impression to staff, to potential customers, and almost inevitably to potential creditors who come around asking for the money you've frittered away on unnecessary things that the business doesn't need.

If you've had a good year, where should you invest your money? I would suggest you invest in the things that generated the extra money in the first place. Spend your money on improving customer care, advertising in publications that worked for you, or on new staff who could continue the good work done by your existing people.

By spending money when you have it on the things that matter, you only increase the long-term overall profitability of your business. By spending it on things that give you the perceived trappings of success, you can often end up undermining the very success that you are hoping to demonstrate to others.

> **Economy does not lie in sparing money but in spending it wisely."**
>
> *–Thomas Huxley*

28

KEEP STUDYING YOUR AREA OF EXPERTISE AND OTHER AREAS OF BUSINESS THAT WILL HELP YOU TO GROW

ONE OF THE reasons that businesses fail to reach their potential is because they rest on their laurels. They have one successful product or service, or one surprise success, but then fail to follow through the success into other areas or markets.

If you want your business to grow in the long term, do not allow it to stagnate. Always look for new ideas, new markets and new approaches to all aspects of your business. It therefore makes sense that you continue to build your personal expertise in elements of the business you have found successful in the past. For example, if you are the financial controller of your company, you should be continually looking at other successful businesses and how they operate. What structures, ideas and innovations can you learn from them? If your area of expertise is sales and marketing, then continually refining and learning about new ways to promote your company and how to close more sales is always going to pay handsome dividends.

The most successful companies are the ones which continually reinvent themselves and encourage their staff to learn new skills. This works for two reasons.

First of all, most good staff are always looking to improve their skills and to learn new areas of expertise. Therefore if you look after their inner hunger to improve themselves, then you are more likely to retain them within your company.

The second reason is that regardless of whether you are learning and innovating or not, you can be certain that your competitors are. Even industries that seem to have scarcely changed in decades can be wiped out almost overnight when an aggressive competitor launches, using new technology. We all need to be ever-vigilant over new technological trends which may either replace what we're currently doing, or which could be a new and successful route to market.

Finally on this point, while it is good to have a general understanding of many aspects of business, it is always good to have a specialisation. If a number of staff working in your company specialised in different and complementary areas, you can quickly produce a 'mastermind' team that is able to tackle many different problems and challenges quickly and effectively. However, don't assume that because you were once a brilliant source of knowledge on a subject that this will always be the case.

ALASTAIR CAMPBELL

29

CREATE A SYSTEM FOR GATHERING TESTIMONIALS FROM SATISFIED CUSTOMERS

I WAS TALKING to a client about testimonials one morning. He explained that over the years he had received many warm letters from customers thanking him for his work. He reached into a drawer and presented me with a folder.

His business involves carrying out the work in people's homes. After the work is completed he sends an invoice and customers post him a cheque within a 14-day period. Many people had written mainly small notes expressing gratitude, and included them with their cheque. Given that he undertook several hundred jobs a year, the total number of testimonials and thank you notes probably represented one in 100 jobs that he had carried out.

One note of thank you for every hundred jobs completed does not in itself mean that he was doing a bad job. Far from it. In fact, he has an excellent reputation in the town and was a very well-respected business. It does, however, show how few people will take the time to write testimonials for the work you have carried out for them.

At this time we were in the process of updating his website. I suggested that a series of rolling testimonials on each page through the site would give a sense of confidence to a prospective customer. We therefore decided to actively seek testimonials from his customers.

The way that we did this was quite simple. We included with the invoice a single sheet of paper containing five questions which people could answer on a scale of 1 to 10. They were all linked to their direct experience of his work. For example, had the workmen turned up on time, had they done a good job, did they represent good value for money etc. At the bottom of this piece of paper was the option to write a comment that summed up what the company had done for them.

For two months, these questionnaires were sent out with every invoice. The next time we met, he showed me the new testimonials that he had received. In the two-month period, he had collected more testimonials than he had in the previous 20 years of business.

Was it because he had become much better over that period? Unlikely. I think it's fairly clear that it was because people were asked their opinions at a time when they were going to be contacting him anyway. It gave people a genuine chance to complain if they were unhappy about any aspect of the service just as they were about to pay for it. It also gave them a chance to say thank you for the work that had been carried out.

It's only right to point out that not everybody completed the form, and not everybody who completed the form wrote a positive testimonial on the bottom of it, even if they had said positive things in the form. Some people are too busy or too uninterested to help you. And that is fine. It doesn't mean they don't like you, it just means they haven't taken the time and trouble to fill out the form. We found around one-third of his customers completed the form and about half of those gave a positive testimonial. However, because of the volume of work that was carried out, this resulted in plenty more testimonials than we actually needed for the website.

You may not be able to copy this model exactly, but think about ways that you can ask your customers for testimonials when they're most likely to give them to you. It might be when you're in a face-to-face meeting with them; or it might be at the end of an event such as a seminar where you are about to close and they are all in the room already. It may be when they are waiting for something to be signed for. There is no end of opportunities to ask people to write a testimonial. The point is that you find some way, during your day-to-day operations, to ask. If you don't, you too will probably end up with only a small number over a 20-year period. Just by asking, you could have more testimonials that you need.

You can never have too many testimonials!

30

YOUR COMPANY SHOULD BE CONTINUALLY IMPROVING EVERY MONTH

WHAT IS your company doing this month that is different from what it did last month? The Japanese business philosophy of 'kaizen' literally means continual improvement. It means looking at what your company does and, rather than scrapping important aspects of that, looking at little improvements that could be made here and there which over time will have a dramatic improvement on how your business functions.

It seems to be almost the opposite of the way that a newly elected government will act. So every five years or so, we have upheaval within the education, housing or benefits systems which experience tells us will only just have started to work when we go to the polls and a new major upheaval arrives.

So is gradual improvement a good idea? Let's look at how this would work in our bodies.

If we overeat by a few hundred calories each day, by the end of the month we might put on one pound in weight. A few pounds in weight gain won't be noticed by anybody, but if the process is continued week in week out – just 200 extra calories per day – then the average person will gain over a stone in weight over the course of a year. Carrying on like this over five years would certainly be noticed.

Of course the opposite – 200 calories less than you need every day – would have the opposite effect. But instead people tend to go on crash diets followed by holiday blowouts, and their weight fluctuates accordingly.

In business it is very easy to get into slightly bad habits. Slightly bad habits are not the end of the world, but they put us on a slightly wrong path. For example, if you get into the habit of drinking the cup of coffee and reading the paper for half an hour every morning when you first get to your desk, how does this set you up productively for the rest of the day? Assuming you do this every day and you work five days a week, 48 weeks of the year, this one seemingly innocuous habit would result in 120 wasted hours every year, or three full working weeks!

All over your business, there could be small time-wasting activities, inefficient practices, and outdated procedures. While it is impossible to improve all of these overnight, if you are always vigilant and look for ways to sharpen things up just a little bit, then over time this approach can have a dramatic overall improvement on your company's productivity. Simple things like setting goals, investigating what your competitors are doing, or ensuring systems and efficient programmes are set up in the company will improve your company's performance dramatically.

31

THINK BACK TO WHAT HAS ALREADY WORKED FOR YOU IN THE PAST

HOW DID you win your best customers? Are you still engaged in that type of marketing activity?

It's amazing how many companies win many of their early customers using one particular type of marketing, but then as time goes on, ditch it for more expensive options. "We once ran seminars to attract new business people," someone will tell me, "but now we advertise in the leading trade magazine at £2,000 a month." Does the advert in the trade magazine produce as many enquiries? No, they say, but it takes less time to do.

In the early days of your business, you had to think on your feet. You perhaps didn't have much of a marketing budget – so you spent it on running low-cost events to reach people, or handing out flyers or one of dozens of low-cost marketing activities that worked for you. They won your first few customers and enabled you to build the business.

So as an exercise now, take 10 minutes with a blank piece of paper and think back to those earlier times. Perhaps a time at a previous company where you have worked. What marketing activities did they do to generate new business enquiries? What were the systems they had in place to convert customers successfully? Not all of them will be appropriate today for you, but perhaps a dilution of them could be adapted to provide an effective low-cost marketing tool that could win new business for you.

It is very easy to dismiss things we once used simply because we have moved on. However in a lot of cases those simple methods proved to be very effective and we stopped doing them, not because they didn't work any more, but because we forgot about them. By reactivating just one of these earlier low-cost strategies, you could open up a stream of new business enquiries that are not possible through your current marketing activities.

32

DON'T RELY ON WORDS ALONE

WORDS ARE incredibly important in marketing your business: don't get me wrong. However photographs and video can connect with people's emotions faster that words can and can draw in people and prompt them to find out more.

It is important to understand that the thoughts and feelings of people can be an extremely valuable tool in persuading potential customers to try your business for the first time. We have all heard the expression that a picture is worth a thousand words. In my opinion, that depends a great deal on the picture, but the right picture or video clip can certainly create a shortcut to people's emotions that would take thousands of words to capture.

Quoted directly in their entirety with the name of the person who said the comments, testimonials can be very persuasive. In fact, clustering together a number of comments, each of which overcomes a major objection to buying from you, can be a very effective marketing tool.

One stage on from the testimonial is a case study. The case

study takes the written word of the individual, and sets up the context of the specific benefits your company or product has been able to offer to this real customer. Again this is very powerful and is widely used, particularly for services which are less tangible than items.

The only problem with testimonials or quotes presented in this way is that they are factual, rather than emotional. In a business-to-business context or within a formal proposal this is the norm.

A great way to stand out from the competition is to use, if possible, a photograph of the person who made the comment. If this is not possible – and it often isn't – you can use a library photograph or generic photograph of the type of person who might have made the comment.

The most impactful alternative is a short testimonial video in which satisfied customers talk about their experiences. For reasons of cost, it is usually best to get several customers to come to the same location where the lights and camera are already set up. Because you are able to see the person talking, or listen to them and the emotion in their voice, the comments come across as far more real and believable and in 60 seconds of material you can create a real emotional connection in the potential customer that is far harder to create through the printed word alone. You are not just looking at the words, you are hearing the emotions in their voice and seeing them on their face.

Such a testimonial video is a surprisingly powerful and persuasive tool to persuade prospects. If you have a good product to sell and you are able to collect and professionally edit such comments together in an entertaining way, so much the better.

33

ASK YOUR CUSTOMERS WHAT THEY LIKE AND DON'T LIKE ABOUT YOUR COMPANY

IT IS VERY easy to assume that we know what customers like and don't like about our products or services. However, we are often the last people to know the truth about our business. In fact, the further you are up the business ladder, and the further away from the day-to-day dealings with customers, the more difficult it is to get a true understanding of customer experiences.

McDonald's recognises this and puts their theory into practice when taking on new management staff. They insist everybody spends time serving in a McDonald's restaurant to give them a strong sense of serving the customer and dealing with customer enquiries. In fact, even staff working for McDonald's advertising agencies have to go through a similar learning experience.

It is a worthwhile thing to send out regular customer surveys asking people what they like and what they don't like about your business. While some people may appear overly critical, or some people too polite to criticise, overall you will get a sense of what you're doing well and, more importantly, what you're doing badly.

ALASTAIR CAMPBELL

It is better to deal with criticism from a customer at an early stage than to carry on thinking you're doing a great job, only to lose a customer because of a small matter that could have been easily overcome.

The simplest way to find out what customers really think of your business is to ask them in a questionnaire where they are able to rate services on a scale of 1 to 10 and leave specific comments about your company. You may not always like the answers you get back – in fact you may not even agree with some of the feedback that you receive – but if a cumulative effect of it is to bring home the unpleasant truth that some aspects of the business could be improved, it is bitter pill that is worth swallowing.

34

ASK YOUR EX-CUSTOMERS WHY THEY LEFT

A METAPHOR that I sometimes use during my seminars is that of the 'business bath'. Imagine that the water coming from the taps is the new business coming into your company and the plug hole represents customers who are leaving. If you have your plug in place, your bath could rapidly fill up. With the taps running and the bath filling, your business is clearly doing well.

In fact, a great deal of marketing effort is spent on working out how to turn the taps on more effectively. Much less effort is spent on working out how to ensure that the plughole is carefully sealed to reduce the number of customers leaving.

One of the best ways I know of minimising the number of customers who leave starts by simply asking ask ex-customers what made them go to a competitor, and to act on what they tell you.

By asking this question every time somebody moves on, or even going back retrospectively and asking past customers if they could remember why they stopped using your services, you could discover an absolute treasure trove of ways to improve your business.

Customers choose to leave for many reasons, from inappropriate opening hours to poor service, to an unfavourable pricing structure, outdated products and everything imaginable in between. If you find you get 100 different small reasons why people leave, you may struggle to put them all right. However, in my experience it is often a limited area which is normally responsible for the majority of departing customers. The 80:20 rule often applies in such circumstances: 80 per cent of the customers who leave could be retained because they are unhappy about the same 20 per cent part of your business. In many cases, these problems can be quickly and inexpensively overcome. Often the problem is down to the perception of customers rather than the reality of the situation. Find out why they are leaving and you can rapidly plug the drain hole to reduce the number of customers who become ex-customers.

While you will never achieve 100 per cent customer retention, it can be surprisingly simple and inexpensive to improve aspects of your business to reduce the number of customers who leave.

35

DISCOVER YOUR DANGEROUS
TIME-WASTING HABITS

BAD HABITS cost money. Nobody is perfect, and we all indulge in simple time-wasting habits that cost our business money. One thing that all business owners can do is to spend valuable time, at least once a month, to examine ways that we could reduce unnecessary waste of time in a company.

I was speaking to a colleague at a recruitment company recently. She placed large numbers of temporary staff in a factory outlet run by one of her clients. While the client thought this company was run smoothly and efficiently, the temporary staff would regularly report back that as much as one-third of their time was wasted every day because the production line in the factory was badly laid out. They talked about having to walk from one end of the factory to the middle then to the start in order to continue a smooth process. People were standing around waiting for work to do and others would get lost on the way across the labyrinthine layout of the old factory setting.

While it wasn't a simple process to rip out a fixed layout, by taking time to plan the factory more carefully (the shutdown might have taken a week) it would have saved many hours of wasted production on a daily basis.

We may not all face such an obvious problem in our companies, but we all have holes in our procedures that could be repaired to enable a smooth operation of the business. In his book *The e-Myth*, Michael Gerber talks about the importance of spending time working on your business, rather than working in the business. We all know the expression to 'work smarter rather than to work harder', but how many of us give this idea more than lip service?

If you can, look at how you spend your time daily and think about the ways that it could have been spent better. How many personal phone calls did you make? How many non-business websites did you surf? How many tasks do you start, do a little bit of work on, then start something else, then put to one side without making any real progress? Look at all the things you do daily and see if there is a pattern emerging which is ultimately costing you hours of wasted time.

By taking a certain amount of time out of your day-to-day business, you can look at the whole problem areas within your company and see those ways of improving productivity and efficiency and focus to ensure that you and your key staff are spending time working more productively than you currently are.

36

PRODUCE GOOD QUALITY BUT DON'T OBSESS OVER MAKING EVERYTHING 'PERFECT'

SOME PEOPLE demand perfection. That is, they will keep changing artwork again and again until in their view it is absolutely perfect and can't be made any better.

One person's perfection is another person's procrastination.

I have worked with clients who rewrite or redesign items so many times that each new revision ceases to be an improvement and instead becomes just a terrible waste of their time and resources.

Take advertising. The most important thing about an advert is that the central idea is strong, the main benefit is put across well, and the overall layout makes it easy to read and understand. While carefully polishing the text is without doubt important, sometimes people will change words just for the sake of changing words.

When an advert meets its criteria and has been carefully proofread, it should be ready to go. However, I have known clients to change very small details in the text up to 20 times, costing a great deal of money in additional design fees rather than accepting when an advert is good enough to run.

I'm not suggesting that half-finished adverts or badly designed or written adverts should go to press – far from it. However, there comes a time when an advert (and the same thing goes for a report or website) is good enough. It is good enough to see whether it will generate money for your company. If it doesn't work as well as you had hoped, it can always be refined and improved at a later stage. But endlessly writing and rewriting copy in the hope of reaching some kind of unattainable perfection is more about procrastination than achieving the ultimate.

For example, when is the video finished? The answer is when it tells the message you wanted to tell. You could spend forever editing and re-editing a piece, grading the colour, adding additional soundtrack, putting in new captions, changing the colour of captions; perhaps you'll be shooting some aspects of the film. When would it be ready? The answer is you could carry on re-editing a piece of film the rest of your life and still not be 100 per cent satisfied.

The truth is most videos are finished editing when editing time runs out in the suite that it is booked for. In those circumstances, people look at it and say it's good enough. If they had the editing facility at home, perhaps it would never be good enough and therefore never finished.

An unfinished video which sits on your computer at home is never going to generate income for your business. Surely it is better to release a video with a strong idea and a clear message that is slightly rough at the edges than to release no video at all.

37

TEST EVERYTHING YOU DO TO SEE WHAT WORKS ABOUT IT AND WHAT DOESN'T

ONE OF THE great advantages of direct marketing is that you can test out different headlines, approaches, offers and in fact anything else to see how you can fine-tune and improve it. If you have a direct mail letter which is currently generating a five per cent response rate, there are so many different aspects that you can change which could double or triple that response rate. Unfortunately most people don't do this. They will take a letter that doesn't work and stop sending it, or take a letter that does work and carry on sending it but not explore the other possibilities that it offers.

Look into different versions of a headline, for example. You would be surprised how much a response rate could be increased. I once changed just three words of the headline and doubled the response rate. Another time, I added a new offer to a letter, and tripled the response rate. By changing the name of a free report that was offered in a letter, I quadrupled the response rate.

How do you know which aspects of the change that you are

making are effective? The answer is to be careful to only change one thing at a time. Change two things and you'll never know which one has made a real difference. So only change one aspect of the headline, offer or a new PS, or change the main body copy.

With direct mail letters, there is a clear order of preference for the different components that can be changed. The biggest change you can make is to the headline. The second biggest change is to the offer that the letter is making. The third biggest change is the PS at the end of the letter and generally the fourth biggest change is to the main copy in the body of the letter itself. This is assuming that all aspects of the letter make sense, are clear and are reasonably well written.

You can test e-mails along similar lines and of course apply the results of the response rates you achieve from e-mails or direct-mail letters across other aspects of your marketing. If a particular appeal in a direct-mail letter worked well, then it can be adapted into the headline of a brochure, website, or even an article pitch to editors.

Never give up testing – use it whenever you can and see how you can fine-tune and improve your marketing results.

38

ONLY SELL PRODUCTS OR SERVICES THAT YOU BELIEVE IN

IF YOU DON'T think the products or services you are selling are excellent, how can you communicate your enthusiasm to your customers?

It has been said that selling is the transfer of enthusiasm for a product from one person to another. Do you believe in the product that you are selling? Do you think it offers good value for money? Do you think it is safe? Would you use the product yourself or recommend it to members of your family?

If the answer to any of those was a resounding no, perhaps you should look at either setting up a different company or working for a different business.

I firmly believe that if you cannot see the real benefits of the product or service your company offers, and you don't believe that your company is an honourable and decent business, then you should move aside and let somebody else take your job.

In our early years at the Ideal Marketing Company, I once took a job for a set of products that I simply did not believe in. I spent one day on the project in total, writing the best copy I could, to run on their website. It was purgatory. More to the point, it was much more difficult than it should have been. I vowed I would never again work for a client that I didn't believe in.

There's a difference between that and working for companies who market a product that I personally wouldn't use. But that is only because I am not in the market for that type of goods or services. For example, we have a client who markets a product to the building industry. I have no need to ever use that product myself. However, I wouldn't have a moment's hesitation in recommending it to a friend who works in the construction industry because, having seen the product demonstrated, I can see a clear benefit for people within the industry.

If you work for a company whose product doesn't work, is dangerous, or is ridiculously over-inflated in price, then it is very difficult to try to sell or market that product. You have to believe the product or service you are marketing has a genuine benefit to the customers; otherwise you will turn yourself into a liar – and nobody likes to think of themselves as a liar.

39

DO MORE OF WHAT YOU ARE PASSIONATE ABOUT AND DELEGATE WHAT YOU CAN'T DO OR HATE DOING

IF I TOLD you that I was great at everything I do, would you believe me? You would be wrong if you did. There are so many aspects of business that I am absolutely hopeless at I don't think I could list them all. There are however some areas that I would like to think I am very good at.

I am good at coming up with ideas, I'm good at thinking quickly, coming up with campaign slogans, thinking visually, writing copy that flows, and a number of other things that modesty prevents me from telling you about.

However, if I was in charge of the company's book-keeping and accounts, I would properly have been in prison for the last six years. I'm not great at some aspects of attention to detail, either. If I think I know what a sentence says, I will often see that rather than what it really says, so I like to get a second opinion on much of my work.

The important thing is to recognise what you do well and do more of it. At the same time, it's good to be aware of your limitations, what you do badly, and ask somebody else to look after that for you.

Too many people pour a huge amount of time and effort into doing something they do badly – to do it slightly better. There is probably a reason why you are doing it badly. You may get better at it, but it's often easier to delegate the task to somebody else who enjoys doing it.

If you find that you are excellent at doing things in your job, the more you do them, the better you will get and the more you will enjoy your work. Conversely, if there's something you're not very good at, chances are you don't enjoy it; and the more you do those things, the more frustrated you'll become in your job.

Quite simply, if you want to enjoy your job more, focus on the things that you find agreeable to do and do them more often. Then find somebody else who loves doing the stuff that you don't enjoy and get them to focus on their job. You will find productivity and enjoyment goes up and, as important, the quality of your company's output goes up at the same time.

40

FIND WAYS TO KEEP INSPIRED

DO YOU GO into work every day whistling a merry tune, thinking 'Hooray, I can spend the next eight hours sitting at my desk looking at a computer screen!' No, I thought not. We all have good days and we almost certainly have bad days when we would rather be someplace else.

There are, no doubt, certain things that inspire you. It may be taking a break and thinking about where you were going on holiday, but for most people, inspiration comes from thinking inspiring thoughts or thinking about inspiring people.

I used to work in an office which was a 35-minute drive from my house. On the journey, I could choose to listen to the radio or a music CD, or I could choose to listen to motivational CDs from companies such as Nightingale Conant or Audible.co.uk. Most the time I chose the latter. That meant for 40 minutes before starting work, I would hear interesting insights into business and marketing from people such as Brian Tracy, Earl Nightingale, or Steve Chandler.

It is always a good idea to go to bed and wake up in the company of thoughts that inspire you. So perhaps reading a book which motivates you first thing in the morning will work for you.

There are plenty of services which will send you a daily motivational tape to start the day with. Or buy desk calendars which have an inspiring thought that will be one of the first things you'll see when you start the day.

It is very easy to sleep-walk through our lives. Taking time out to find ways that motivate us can be a very worthwhile investment in time.

When we get into a slump, even thinking about making positive changes seems too difficult. But it's not hopeless: with some small steps, baby ones in fact, you can get started down the road to positive change."

−Leo Babauta

41

WATCH YOUR ENERGY LEVELS AND OVERALL HEALTH

VOLTAIRE SAID 'Tiredness makes cowards of us all.' You may not have realised it, but often when everything becomes too much in our lives, it is because we are either ill or tired. Having low energy levels makes even day-to-day tasks seem too much for us to even think about it.

If you want to achieve more in your everyday life, the first starting point is your own body and mind. You would not expect a badly treated car with hardly any petrol, a flat battery and no oil to perform at its peak. The same is true with our bodies. By looking after our daily diet and exercise routines, it's amazing how much extra energy we can give ourselves.

One thing that most of us find surprising is that by doing regular exercise, we don't feel more tired – we actually feel more energetic. Another great thing about exercise is the more you do it, the more you want to do it, and the easier it becomes.

Many years ago, when I was in my 20s, I gave up smoking. At the same time, I decided I would start running. We were living in

Pimlico, central London, where many blocks of flats are in box-like grids similar to New York. My first run couldn't have been longer than half a mile, but by the time I got back to the flat, I felt that my lungs had bust outside of my body. I was absolutely exhausted and probably couldn't have run any further even if my life depended on it. However, I persevered and did the same run every day for a week. By the start of the second week, this short run seemed very easy indeed, and I decided to extend it. Less than two years later, I had completed my first London Marathon.

Exercise is a good habit to develop and an amazing thing if you do it on a regular basis.

The same applies food. So much of what we eat gives us very little nutritional value and only generates calories which, in turn, turn into pounds. By reducing our calorie intake and increasing the amount of exercise we do, we can very rapidly lose weight.

I lost two stone in two months. All I did was follow a diet of 1,000 calories a day – and I was very strict, cutting out all chocolate, biscuits, cakes and puddings while increasing my exercise with running up to 12 miles a day. The result was, perhaps not surprisingly, rapid weight loss. The interesting thing is, because I had a very clear goal in mind about how much weight I wanted to lose and when I wanted to lose it by, I found the process not only enjoyable but surprisingly easy.

You may not wish to lose weight, but if you want to increase your energy levels, the best way to do so is to watch what you eat and exercise more. Large meals and rich puddings, besides the calories, are one of the simplest ways of sending us to sleep.

Watch what you eat and decide to exercise regularly and over time the results are dramatic.

42

ENTER AWARDS AND DISPLAY YOUR TROPHIES WHERE PEOPLE WILL SEE THEM

WHO WOULD you prefer to work with: a company which has won awards, has enthusiastically learned from its customers, and supports community or industry activities, or a company that does none of those things?

Most of us would like to work with companies which are clearly doing good work.

Interestingly, a lot of companies I speak to have either been nominated for or won awards, but they feel almost embarrassed to display a sign of achievement. Similarly, many companies I know have received glowing testimonials from customers but do nothing with them. And again, companies support local children's football and rugby teams or other community-based organisations but don't seem to mention it to their customers or even their staff.

While telling people of your accomplishments will not necessarily generate new enquiries, it will help to convert sales as potential customers admire companies which have achieved something with their business.

If you have a presentation room, sales meeting room or indeed any space in the company where prospects will come to meet you, it is a good idea to put some time and thought into the sorts of displays you have on your walls. A reproduction of a Constable painting may set the scene, but is unlikely to close that business. Better to display certificates, trophies, photographs and other images showing a dynamic, forward-thinking company that is recognised either by the industry or the local community.

It's surprising the effect that positive images such as this will have on your prospects. Everybody likes dealing with successful companies, and if you can demonstrate clearly that you are a successful business, people will be keener to deal with you than your competitors.

These days there are awards for almost everything. Customer service awards, local business awards, industry awards: you name it, there is an award for it. Some awards are unbelievably difficult to get because they are highly contested and judged to an astonishingly high standard. However there are plenty of awards which not many people enter.

A friend of mine recently received a runner-up award in an environmental category for a regional business award scheme. He came second, but from a catchment area with a population of almost one million people, guess how many companies entered this category? Two. But he still got certificates, was invited to the awards dinner and has a photograph of him receiving the award in front of a crowd of 300 people.

Many people imagine that entering awards takes up too much time. In fact, many awards are designed to be relatively simple to enter. You will also find that judges will often ask for similar types of information. That means entering two awards won't take twice the time it takes to enter one award. And entering the same award the following year will often take not much more time at all because you can use a lot of the research you did the first year.

A lot of people don't enter awards because they don't like the thought of not winning. The truth is that if you aren't shortlisted, nobody will know that you even entered. And if you are shortlisted but on the night you don't win the award, your company will still be named within the top three companies in that area. You might not win, but it shows clearly that you're one of the top companies in the industry or area simply by being nominated and getting to the final. There is no shame in being a finalist for the award and being pipped at the post.

Finding out about awards you can enter involves a simple trawl of the internet. It may surprise you just how many different business awards there are. Take some time to look around and you will discover awards for everything from people development to the environment and beyond. If you are not an award-winning company now, you certainly can be in the next 12 months if you focus your mind in the task.

ALASTAIR CAMPBELL

43

FIND PEOPLE YOU TRUST TO GIVE YOU IDEAS AND ADVICE

NOBODY ACHIEVES great things all by themselves. They may come up with the idea and be the leader of the project, but 'no man is an island'. Nobody in the world knows everything already. And certainly nobody who has reached any level of success has achieved it on their own.

Even the most intelligent of individuals require help from other people. In the Oscar-winning film *The Social Network*, which traces the rise of Facebook, it is clear that although one person was the driving force behind the business, many others were involved at the every stage whether it was for their inspiration, finance or practical input.

But sometimes it is a good idea to find an individual or group of individuals whose opinion is independent from the outcome. The idea of having a board of directors to scrutinise, question and review decisions and outcomes of your company is a well established practice. But who is there to do the equivalent action with your whole life?

The growth in popularity of life coaching on both sides of the Atlantic is interesting. It shows the value placed in a monthly session with an independent minded individual to assess the progress you've made of the previous four weeks.

There are other methods.

The buddy system: Is there somebody who you respect and admire - and who respects and admires you – who you could meet on a regular basis? The idea is to set up either phone calls or person-to-person meetings where you put aside a certain amount of time to examine how you have both got on over the previous month. The simple act of questioning progress made, goals achieved, decisions taken will accelerate our progress to achieving what we want to achieve in our lives. Knowing that at a certain date we will be held to account by a person we respect changes the focus of activities. We become more results driven and look at ways to achieve the targets that we made a personal commitment to meet.

The mastermind group: Using similar principles of the buddy system, the mastermind group typically has up to seven other people who will give you feedback and help you set goals over the coming month. An ideal mastermind group is made up of people who you respect but with whom you don't have a great deal of day-to-day activity. By acting as independent witnesses to how your life is progressing, they give you a clearer picture and will stop you from dodging issues which you may find difficult to handle. They will also be there to answer questions, give expert advice and the benefit of their wisdom. Because you're not listening to just one person's opinion, the effect of the mastermind group can be considerably more powerful than the buddy system – if you get the right people.

The mastermind group approach was first written about in the book *Think and Grow Rich*, by Napoleon Hill. In a study of the wealthiest people in America, he was surprised to learn that most of these industrialists employed this principle to great effect. Many said that they couldn't imagine operating or growing their businesses without using mastermind groups. I can personally testify to the power of these groups; I helped found one in 2005 and have been in it since.

The point is this: accept that we don't have all the answers, and neither does anybody else. But thinking aloud and hearing other people's feedback on where we are and where we think we are going stops us from kidding ourselves that we are achieving more than we are. It's amazing the difference that the reality check of the group of people we admire will make to how we view our lives, and therefore how quickly we can progress the goals that we seek.

44

USE PEOPLE IN YOUR MARKETING MATERIAL (NOBODY WANTS TO EAT IN AN EMPTY RESTAURANT)

IT DOESN'T matter who your target market is, I can promise you one thing: it will be a person (at least at the moment of sale).

People respond to people. As humans, we are programmed to be able to recognise the faces of people we perhaps haven't seen in decades.

Nowadays we still see people around us all the time, in shops, offices and meetings. But for some reason, a lot of companies don't use people in their brochures. Classic examples of this *faux pas* are the photographs you see all the time of restaurants without customers. You'll see this on websites as well: photographs of completely empty restaurants, every seat perfectly aligned but empty and no food in sight.

As a potential customer walking past that restaurant looking in, would you dine there? You see a restaurant on the High Street, you walk over to it and look in the window; there is nobody inside. That tells you at a glance one of two things: it's closed or it's rubbish. Either way, you probably will cross back over the road.

Now imagine a different image: a photograph of a restaurant that is two-thirds full of people and those you can see in the foreground are clearly having a good time. If you were to look through the window and see this scene, would your reaction be different? You might assume that this place must be okay as it is quite busy, and its customers appear to be enjoying themselves. Can you see now why, for a restaurant, it is so important to have the right type of photograph to illustrate its dining room?

But the same is true with almost every type of company brochure I can think of. Whatever is being sold, the addition of people will help to demonstrate the benefits it offers.

If we allow ourselves to focus solely on product, we are in danger of focusing on the features rather than the benefits.

Customers are people and they are the ones who receive the benefits from any product or service that we offer. Showing them enjoying the experience, service or product is a good way to sell more of it.

Always do a 'people check' on any marketing material you produce. Are people in it and if so, do they look as though they are enjoying themselves? If not, perhaps it's time to commission new photography to help create more memorable images which will help attract customers.

Whatever audience you are selling to, there is always a space for people. People on the cover attract customers to turn the page and look inside. People inside trying the product, benefiting from the product – perhaps even a person on the phone ready to take the order – are a good way to prompt potential customers to take action.

45

PUT ACTION INTO YOUR EXHIBITIONS

I HAVE A confession to make. Possibly because of my time as a marketing manager, I have never liked trade shows and exhibitions. Perhaps it is because of the stressful build-up when new literature, case studies, banner stands and so on had to be ready for a specific date. Perhaps it is the endless hours of standing in an airless, windowless environment talking to people who clearly have no interest in your company. Or perhaps it is because, after attending many shows at large national trade events, I was never convinced that they resulted in much new business.

However, I've changed my mind. Now I run my own business and have taken exhibition space for a number of years at smaller events, I now think that they can be very effective if you put the correct preparation and planning into the event.

This is by no means an exhaustive list, but here are some ideas that you might want to use if you are considering taking part in a trade show and exhibition.

Make a splash. If it's possible, ask the organisers if you're able to speak at the event. Many trade shows allow exhibitors the opportunity to speak at seminar sessions during the day. It's a great way to attract people over to your stand either before or after you've spoken. When your session finishes, invite your audience to come over to your stand to pick up a free report, booklet of tips or other useful material based on the talk that you gave at the event.

Give advance warning. Begin by sending out news releases about any new products or services you will be introducing at the trade show. Send them to the appropriate trade magazines because some of the readers are likely to attend and if you have the right product, will make a point of coming to your stand. Also, if there are any trade magazines, TV or radio stations that are present and publishing or broadcasting at the event, gaining a prominent position with a good story will attract people along to your stand. Remember, the game is about volume – get as many people visiting you on that day as you can.

Give them something to look at. Not only should your stand look attractive and have some bright eye-catching features about it, I would suggest that having some kind of mobile or interactive element is very worthwhile. I have known companies to hire magicians, singers, acrobats or even clowns which draw in a crowd. Many people will be walking around bored at these events, and if your stand is memorable and gives them something to look at (particularly if it is relevant to the message that you're putting across) you can attract big crowds and gather lots of names of key people. You are unlikely to sell on the day: always remember this. It is an information gathering exercise above all else.

Create a check list. To reduce your stress levels, I'd always recommend creating a check list of what you need to take along to the event. Every time you think of something, add it to the list. That way your last-minute preparation is far less stressful and you won't have the nagging doubt that you have left something behind.

I'm still not always 100 per cent convinced that exhibitions are the right thing for every business, but if you are committed to one that attracts lots of the right people for you, then you should do everything you can to make sure that they swing by your stand and leave their details, rather than just crossing your fingers and seeing what happens.

ALASTAIR CAMPBELL

46

WATCH OUT FOR POOR LANGUAGE WITHIN YOUR ORGANISATION

IF I WERE to mention 'the scum', what would I be talking about? Unfortunately, in the example I'm thinking of, I am not referring to the vegetable matter which rises to the top of soup, or the ring left around the top of a bath. This is what one company calls its customers!

Can you believe that? The people who pay the bill, the business rates and where all the profits come from to pay the staff's wages are referred to as 'the scum'.

Interestingly, this company has had some serious customer relation and retention issues. Is that a surprise? If the culture within a company can allow phrases such as 'the scum' to be attached to the most valuable asset a business possesses, it is no wonder that it gets into trouble.

When the phone rings and a customer is asking a question, what is the general body language of the customer services department? Is it positive and eager to please or is it a different story altogether? Are customers treated as simpletons or morons?

Be careful what standards you allow to develop within your company, particularly in relation to customers and prospects. Always treat customers with respect and if you ever hear people referring to them in less than complimentary terms, ask them if they would rather that customer had used one of your competitors.

This may seem like a small point, but it could be symptomatic of an overall attitude and culture within a company. We should always put the customer at the centre of everything we do. Without the customer there are no holidays and bonuses; no company cars. Everything that we do should be about serving the customer better.

If you allow bad language to creep into our organisation, it can quickly lead to very bad things. Don't create a culture in your company where the customer is looked down upon. Put the customer on a pedestal. Look up to them and let them lead you to a Golden Age. Don't allow negative members of staff to drag you into your own Dark Ages.

ALASTAIR CAMPBELL

47

METAPHORS ARE A GREAT WAY TO EXPLAIN DIFFICULT OR COMPLEX IDEAS

IF I WERE to ask you to imagine a hippopotamus skating on the ice with a trifle balanced on its head, the chances are you could picture that almost straight away. That's because we are able to understand complicated ideas very quickly if we can see them as pictures.

In fact, speaking of the hippopotamus, a well-known mattress manufacturer has very successfully used a picture-based metaphor in its advertising campaign for a number of years. Silent Night uses a hippopotamus and a chick in bed together. Whatever you may think of the implications of this for cross-species relations, it makes a very strong point about how their mattress doesn't cause them to roll together because of the technology involved in its springs. We equate the hippopotamus with heavy, and the chick with light. So rather than going on at great length about how the technology used in this mattress enables light and heavy people to sleep together, it uses a dramatic metaphor of heavy and light so that we can understand and remember.

Metaphors in advertising are a way of quickly cutting to the point. With TV commercials mostly lasting 30 seconds or less and press adverts holding the reader's eye for seconds at best, we need to help our audience quickly grasp the point that we are putting across.

Is something very fast? Use a picture of rocket. Are there great savings involved? How about a wheelbarrow full of cash? Is something very simple to understand? How about someone sitting in the corner with a pointed hat carrying a giant letter 'D' on it?

If you are looking for a way to explain the benefits of your product, metaphors – and in particular, simple visual metaphors – are a great way to do it. How will your product help people? How will it make them feel? How much time will it save them and what will they do with it all? How will they feel after they have used it compared with before they used it? All of these problems and solutions can be simply presented as visual metaphors.

By creating metaphors around our products, we can not only explain faster what the advantages of it are, we can also create a visual hook which helps people remember a product, a solution or a benefit.

48

MAKING ANY DECISION IS USUALLY BETTER THAN MAKING NO DECISION

HOW DO YOU know when you have just made the right decision? The truth is you may never know – or at least not for many years.

There is an old Chinese proverb about Sai Weng and his horse. Sai Weng lived on a farm near the border of China and Mongolia. He was a keen equestrian and very proud of his horse. It was his pride and joy, but then one day the horse died in a freak accident. A neighbour felt sorry for him and cursed his back luck, but Sai Weng didn't believe in luck. "It's not necessarily bad luck," he said, "we'll have to see."

After awhile Sai Weng decided to buy another horse, but the first time he rode it, the animal bolted, throwing Sai Weng who broke his leg in the fall. The neighbour was quick to comment on the terrible bad luck that Sai Weng was experiencing. "It's not necessarily bad luck," Sai Weng said, "we'll have to see."

Two weeks later a Chinese Army commander came to the village. All the young men had to go to war against Mongolia. But Sai Weng was unable to go because of his broken leg. Less than a month later all the men were dead – killed in a terrible battle. Sai Weng reflected on what this taught him about the nature of luck and decision making. Often what would appear to be bad luck turns out to be good and what seems to be a bad decision turns out for the best in the end. We can only tell which is which over a very long time.

Of course we make hundreds of tiny decisions every day. If we agonised forever over each one, the chances are we would be paralysed with fear. A trip on the motorway could lead to a car crash and a meal in a restaurant could give you food poisoning. Everything that we do has potential positive and negative consequences. And if things go wrong, very often this is because of something that we never could have predicted.

Large organisations, especially public bodies such as councils, seem terrified of making any decision for fear of doing the wrong thing. Politicians, when faced with an unpopular decision (such as pension reform or social security changes), will do anything to make it appear the decision was in fact forced upon them – often, it seems, by a committee that they appointed in the first place. They will set up royal commissions, independent reviews, anything to kick a decision into the next parliament.

Small business owners don't have the luxury of indecision. We need to act quickly – make a decision and then move on.

The best way to achieve results is to weigh up the pros and cons and then arrive at a conclusion with speed. Sometimes you should consult a wise and valued colleague, sometimes you need to reflect on past experiences, and sometimes you will want to reflect back on how other people might have handled a hypothetical situation. But don't get so bogged down in all the alternatives that you put off a decision until it's too late. Your staff will respect your decisive leadership, your ability to get the key facts from a situation and then make a sound and swift judgement. Develop the habit of making decisions quickly. In fact, this is one of the key skills to develop which ultimately will determine how successful you will become.

Surprisingly few decisions really make that much difference in the long run – or if they do, it is due to circumstances beyond your control. Do you merge with this company or that one? Do you hire this job applicant or another one? Do you locate in this town or that town? On one level, these are all massive decisions but who is really to know if they are correct for years to come?

A highly promising salesperson might develop bad habits in the long term because he falls in love with his next door neighbour – but would you really be able to predict that behaviour from an interview? One town may start offering reductions in business rates five years down the line because a major employer went bust – but honestly, would you be able to guess that would happen?

In truth all we can do is look at the facts at the time, weigh up the known pros and cons, and then make a clear decision. If you don't, everything and everybody will be left in a state of limbo waiting for you to make up your mind.

We all learn from our mistakes; we learn from the things that didn't work out. Often people will tell us valuable and useful information which we will completely ignore because, until we've made the mistake for ourselves, we can't actually learn from it.

So don't stop making a decision for fear of one day making the wrong one. You'll make lots of 'wrong' decisions every day but the world keeps on turning. The truth is that as long as you make a decision and follow through with it to the best of your ability, more often than not it will turn out okay, even if in some ways it was probably the wrong decision. When you're paralysed with fear and end up making no decisions – that's when things really start to go wrong in your business.

> "When you have to make a choice and don't make it, that is in itself a choice."
>
> – William James

49

ENTER INTO JOINT VENTURES WITH RELATED BUT NON-COMPETING BUSINESSES

SO YOU'VE decided that a great market for you is people who drive the Ford Ka. You have invented a special product which can be inserted into the fuel tank of a Ford Ka that reduces petrol consumption by up to 50 per cent. You obviously generate a certain amount of PR around this idea, and you advertise it in the general newspapers. But one of the best ways to promote the product would be as a joint venture with related but non-competing businesses.

In this particular case, it could be garages that service the Ford Ka. Garages have contact details for their customers, including which of them drive that particular model. Will their customer be interested in the modification? A good number of them will be. So you go to the garage and offer to do a joint promotion. The letter, which would come from the garage, would say:

Dear customer
You may have heard about the remarkable new product

> which can save up to 50 per cent of fuel consumption in the Ford Ka. We have investigated this product, and can confirm that it not only exists, but it does what it claims with no damage to your car.
> We would like to invite you to bring your car into our garage where we can fit it on your car for a nominal fee. This will result in substantial fuel savings and the cost of fitting will typically be paid back within a matter of days. You can either get the item fitted at your next scheduled service with us, or you could bring interested in there with a special price of X pounds.

Can you see how effective this letter would be? Because the customer's trusted garage has contacted them directly, you don't have to build up a relationship – this joint venture has created a quick route to instant trust. You have piggybacked onto their exiting relationship.

In order to work out who would make a suitable joint partner, you need to decide who you are trying to target within the marketplace. Small business owners? DIY enthusiasts? Chocolate lovers? Each of them already buys from somewhere and if you have a product which is not competitive but complimentary with what their supplier offers, you could create a successful joint venture relationship.

Joint ventures can work in a number of different ways, but the simplest one is agreeing a straightforward profit split. Alternatively you could pay a fixed amount for each lead that you are given, or you could agree to launch a separate company that runs this business separate from your existing companies. Your decision will depend on what appears to be the most appropriate course of action.

Whether you are a business to consumer company, or a business-to-business company, joint ventures can be a fantastically profitable way to generate lots of enquiries very quickly when you're launching a new product into the market and have a clear audience in mind whose needs are partly serviced already by somebody else.

> Hey you, don't tell me there's no hope at all. Together we stand, divided we fall."
>
> – Roger Waters

50
WRITE A BOOKLET OF TIPS

DO YOU HAVE a service-related business? Are you an expert on a particular topic? Do people ask you certain questions on a regular basis? Are you able to help people overcome a particular problem?

I would imagine the answer to all these questions is probably yes. Whether we realise it or not, we are experts in our own area and as result could help customers save, generate or acquire money or time.

A great way to establish expertise and generate leads is to create a tips booklet. Over the years I've written more than a dozen booklets of tips for the Ideal Marketing Company, and I've probably created at least as many again for clients. A tips booklet is usually no more than 1,000 words in total and usually has the number of tips in the title for example:

- 26 Ways to Improve the Response Rate of Your Next Direct-Mail Campaign

ALASTAIR CAMPBELL

- A – Z of Running Better Teams
- 15 Ways to Write a More Effective Press Release
- The 35 Ideas for Creating Better Roast Dinners

Each of these tips booklet titles will appeal to a different person. If I am struggling for PR ideas, then the tips booklet on PR will appeal to me. And as the Ideal Marketing Company, if I am trying to find companies who need help with their PR, what a great way to find companies interested in this area of marketing.

To start with, your tips booklet needs to have a title. Don't worry too much about the numbers of tips you're going to create, although it's probably not a bad idea to have a minimum number in mind. You can use 25 as a starting point – you can always increase or decrease depending on how many tips you come up with.

The title should reflect an area of your business which you're trying to increase. So for example if you have identified that your customer base is people trying to save money on their energy bills, the tips booklet could be titled *25 Ways to Reduce Energy Consumption and Slash Energy Bills*. This title would probably work quite well as a way of generating interest in the tips booklet, and therefore your company.

Now you have come up with a title which you think will entice customers to your business because it solves a problem they are currently experiencing, the next stage is to generate the ideas. If you are a sole trader, or want to write the book yourself, then simply brainstorm ideas that you think will work and write them down. However if you work with other people in your department, here is a great process of quickly writing a tips booklet.

At the end of the next departmental meeting when you are all already assembled and have been talking about ideas to do with the business, explain that in the next five minutes you are going to create a tips booklet to help promote the company. Write down the title of the tips booklet on a white board. Explain what you're trying to do and why you're writing a tips booklet. Then invite everyone in the room to fill a blank piece of paper with their best 10 ideas over the next five minutes.

They don't have to flesh out all the detail of the ideas, simply come up with the idea which will make a one sentence headline. When the time is up, go around the room and see how many ideas people have come up with. You will find that most people are able to come up with at least 10 ideas – many will have come up with more.

Give someone in the department the task of compiling all the ideas onto a single sheet. You will usually find a number of ideas are repeated by different people. By the time the duplicate ideas and the bad ones are weeded out, you may end up with something around 20 to 30. Now look through these ideas. Are there any obvious gaps? Is there a logical sequence that they could be put into? I would always recommend starting with one or two really strong ideas, and finishing on a strong idea too. You may also want to have an idea in quite near the end which is related to your business and what you do.

Now you have them, it's time to flesh out these ideas to a couple of paragraphs in length. You might want to share this job around the various members of the team.

Now you have expanded on the 25 ideas, the next stage is just to write a simple paragraph introduction and a similar conclusion.

Talk to a local printer who can lay out the text and create an attractive front and back cover. Decide how many to print and just sit back and wait. In a matter of just a few hours, you have created a valuable lead generation tool.

Your tips booklet can be given away from your website, when you meet prospects, at networking events or in direct mail campaigns. It can be displayed in your reception area and given to your sales staff to take with them into meetings. It is not only a useful resource for your prospects and a great way of generating enquiries, it is also a great way to establish credibility and knowledge within the market.

> She generally gave herself very good advice, though she very seldom followed it."
>
> –Lewis Carroll

51

REVISIT YOUR PAST CUSTOMERS: THEY ARE A POTENTIAL GOLDMINE

IN MARKETING, you will often hear about potential customers and existing customers. Potential customers are the subject of a great deal of new business activity. Their names are entered into spreadsheets and discussed at monthly sales meetings; they are wooed and wowed by the best people in your company.

Existing customers might not get quite that level of attention once you have managed to convert them, but most good organisations have customer retention programs, account managers and perhaps some personal attention from the MD for the bigger customers.

There is however an important but neglected group of people that can be one of the easiest to convert of all – the ex-customer.

The ex-customer has had some dealings with your business in the past and for whatever reason stopped using you. They may have found a cheaper competitor, they may have forgotten about you, they may be unaware of the scope of your offer or they may simply have lost your contact details.

As business owners, many of us are slightly embarrassed about approaching people who used to deal with us, but don't any more. There may be, in some cases, a clear reason why they stopped using us; a dispute over price or service could mean that neither side wishes to see the other. That's okay if we messed up or if we no longer wish to attract a particular type of customer: strike them off the list and move on. But this type of ex-customer is very much the exception. Most customers simply drift away for no particularly good reason. They don't come back to us, but this is often because we reduce or cease marketing to them – and so they have gone elsewhere.

If you think about it, these people have already experienced some aspects of our business, and so should be among the first to be offered new products, services and special deals to tempt them back.

Do you have a section on your database of ex-customers who you contact regularly? If not, now is a great time to introduce one. Simply letting them know about special offers and events, product launches, samples etc is a great way to re-introduce yourself. You will typically find that conversion rates using targeted campaigns amongst ex-customers are up to five times higher than with non-customers. Why not try it out over the next three months and see what happens?

52

ALWAYS GIVE MORE THAN YOU PROMISED AND LOOK FOR WAYS OF DELIVERING ADDED VALUE

FINALLY, I want to take you to an idyllic scene in a small Greek taverna overlooking the sea. My family and I have enjoyed a wonderful meal and we're sitting looking out to sea as the sun sets. As the waiter clears the plates from the main course, another waiter brings out some home-made Madeira cake, ice cream and fruit. They start putting it down on the table.

"Excuse me," I say, "we didn't order any dessert."

But it turns out that in this town and several others in the area, dessert is a gift from the restaurant owner. They don't have a dessert menu as such, so instead they give you some cake, ice cream or fruit. Sometimes they give you watermelon; other times, they will give you their mother's home-made cake or, as they put it, "something sweet from the cow" – ice cream to us.

We weren't expecting this at the end of a meal and it wasn't a big amount, but that's not the point. It was wonderful finishing touch, an added bonus which really made the meal.

In these competitive days with almost unlimited choice around us, you should always be asking yourself what extra value should you deliver to your clients, prospects and customers? How can you go the extra mile to keep them happy? What can you do that they will remember and appreciate and that may even be the difference between them coming back and recommending you to their friends or choosing a competitor next time round.

In his seminal self-development book *Think and Grow Rich*, Napoleon Hill states that one of the key principles understood by most business owners is that we should always deliver extra value than what we are paid to do. If you are paid for working nine to five and you work those hours, do what is expected of you and no more, how can you expect a promotion or a pay rise? It's only by working longer, smarter or harder, making you worth more than you are currently paid, that security and promotion can be expected.

The same applies in every aspect of life, including growing your business.

The truth is that many companies do okay by being mediocre. You could probably deliver on the basics and make a nice living all of your life.

But who wants to be ordinary? My guess is that you've bought this book because you want to do something above and beyond. You want to grow your business. You want people to come back and recommend what you do to their friends. You want to grow your business, day by day, week by week into an exceptional business that people talk about, remember, think about and want to be associated with. You might not want to be the next Google, Apple or Virgin, but you want to be well respected and good at what you do because it's good to be the best you can be.

One way of being remembered for being great is to deliver on what you promise and a little bit extra. What can you do that is unexpected that will delight customers?

It's the willingness to give that bit extra that people will remember and talk about. That's what will make them keen to come back for more.

If you can dream it, then you can achieve it. You will get all you want in life if you help enough other people get what they want.."

−Zig Ziglar

A PARTING GIFT TO YOU

IF YOU HAVE found this book helpful and want to start introducing some of these ideas to grow your business, I would like to offer you a free, no obligation, one-hour telephone consultation for your business. There is no catch. I will spend an hour on the phone giving you ideas about specific strategies that you can use to help your company grow using these and other low-cost marketing and PR ideas. Just visit The Ideal Marketing Company website to learn how to claim your free marketing consultation.

Regular marketing updates: If you would like to receive monthly updates and tips offering marketing and PR advice as well as news of free and paid for seminars that I run, please sign up for my monthly newsletter. Just e-mail me at *newsletter@idealmarketingcompany.com* or visit our website, *www.idealmarketingcompany.com,* and sign up to receive your monthly newsletter.

ABOUT THE AUTHOR

ALASTAIR CAMPBELL was born in Stirling, Scotland in 1967. He studied Film and Television at Harrow College (now Westminster University) and after graduating, worked for several London advertising agencies during the industry's boom years of the late 1980s and early '90s. During this period he won a national competition for writing a Holsten Pils TV commercial.

After almost 10 years in London with the Pearson-owned Register Group, during which time he rose to become marketing manager, in 1997 he relocated to Leicestershire where, as marketing manager for Lines Unlimited, he helped win business with almost half of the commercial radio stations in the UK. The company won the Marketing Company of the Year Award from the Marketing Guild.

After six years with the group, latterly as head of the marketing and telemarketing departments of the firm's holding company, Voice Connect, Alastair left to set up The Ideal Marketing Company. That was in 2003, and since then, he has worked for clients in sectors as diverse as print, leisure, recruitment, food, education, IT, retail, motorsport, construction, TV, health, training, skiing, retail, insurance, weight loss, food and packaging.

He believes that effective, low-cost marketing ideas should be made to work for every business and spreads this message via his seminars and public speaking engagements which have taken him to the NEC, Olympia, the Walkers Stadium, the MK Dons Stadium, Madejski Stadium, The National Liberal Club in Westminster and Hothorpe Hall. He writes for trade magazines and websites and has been a regular contributor to BBC radio since 2002.

Alastair practises what he preaches, working with clients on a consultancy basis – helping them implement many of the ideas contained in this book. In 2008, he set up The Marketing Mentor programme to help companies with their marketing on an on-going basis by using monthly phone conferences and open question sessions.

Alastair and his wife, Helen (who is a fellow director in the company), have two sons at secondary school. They believe it is important to find a balance between work and home life and admit that it's not always easy.

"Marketing," he says, "is about spending time and thought to be clear about what you are hoping to achieve rather than throwing money at it. Do more of what works for you, but do some marketing activity every week without fail to avoid boom and bust in your company."

This is Alastair Campbell's second book. His first, *The Marketing Launchpad*, was also published by Mosaïque Press.

CONTACT THE AUTHOR

You can contact Alastair directly with feedback, comments or questions at *alastair@idealmarketingcompany.com* or by telephone on +44 (0)1858 44 55 43.

- *www.idealmarketingcompany.com*

www.ingramcontent.com/pod-product-compliance
Lightning Source LLC
Chambersburg PA
CBHW070448090426
42735CB00012B/2489